FIYT CLUB

Finding the Energy to Chase YOUR Dream

RANDY S. ROHRICK

Suite 300 - 990 Fort St
Victoria, BC, V8V 3K2
Canada

www.friesenpress.com

ISBN
978-1-4602-8780-4 (Hardcover)
978-1-4602-8781-1 (Paperback)
978-1-4602-8782-8 (eBook)

1. SELF-HELP

Distributed to the trade by The Ingram Book Company

TABLE OF CONTENTS

"I wish I had..."
The opening of the worst end-of-life statement ever.

This book is dedicated to all who have dreams but live in the fear that they will never find the energy to chase them down.

My hope and prayer is that this book will be the catalyst you need to start, continue, or restart the pursuit of your dreams.

There is something about going after a dream that makes life worth the living. Dream chasing adds color to what can be a black and white existence.

FIYT stands for _F_uel _I_n _Y_our _T_ank

FIYT CLUB is dedicated to assisting people to find ways to fuel their energy tanks.

Check out information and coming events at fiytclub.com

INTRODUCTION

...WHAT GIVES ME THE RIGHT TO WRITE A BOOK ON DREAM CHASING?

Good question.

First of all, I have had a wide range of experience with people from varying ages, backgrounds, cultures, belief systems, and classes. I served as a youth pastor for nine years, working with middle school-aged kids, high schoolers, college students, and young marrieds.

Also, I have performed well over a hundred weddings, come alongside of people in crisis, and buried far too many people who died of everything from cancer and heart attacks, to an airplane crash and a rafting accident. I have buried the old, newborns, and many in between. I'd never be able to recall all the hospital visits I have done over a thirty-five-year span.

I have led numerous "mosaic" style small groups, men's studies, marriage groups, and single/single again groups.

Some of the churches I have been involved in are multicultural and we had ethnic churches we worked with using a common building. This provided some "learning as you go" type interactions. I have had the unique privilege of speaking in places like Bogota, Colombia, Chui, Uruguay, and Boma in the Congo... interpreters included!

A wide range of opportunities has led me to work with churches that had staffs between two and sixty members and staff sizes in between. I have served as lead pastor and have also enjoyed working in other support positions.

Over thirty years I believe I have had and continue to have one of the best jobs on the planet, when it comes to experiencing the best and worst of people. "If you enjoy what you do you never have to work a day in your life." That is the experience of this soul-care specialist...commonly known as clergy; a minister or pastor.

Added to this, my family and I have gone through a good number of roller coaster rides that proved to be an education in and of themselves.

I do have a masters in religious education, but by far, it's the experience of life that has led me to write.

...SO, WHY THIS TOPIC?

Simple. People are tired and feel worn out, yet they are looking to do more than just survive or make it through this thing called life.

It seems like we start well. We have a dream or two we chase. Make some headway. There is some success. And then "life" happens! All of a sudden we find ourselves trying to keep up to the pace of a short-circuited treadmill that is stuck somewhere between fast and stupid fast.

Just ask a couple who has begun a family. Or those further along in life who didn't realize that grown kids still have many time-absorbing needs. Add to that the pressure of keeping an eye on aging parents. This doesn't even touch on personal health challenges, job stresses, and other relational stuff. And then there are the occasional "What is life all about?" moments, which can send us for an interesting ride in and of themselves.

And the list of challenges goes on and on. Our energy tank just doesn't carry us as far as it used to. Somehow we have to fuel up or lose out on any dream we might have had.

At the age of fifty-five, I have learned some things about refueling that might help someone like you. I love where I am in life and I continue the pursuit of my dreams with an energy that I didn't have earlier in life. Often I just didn't fuel up at important times.

This book is not about having it all together. It's about living, learning, and sharing ideas that might spur some on to getting a hold of a dream.

Have fun reading. There might just be a game changer in these pages.

PREAMBLE

THE 1% PRINCIPLE

Throughout my life I have attended a plethora of classes, seminars, conferences, mentoring sessions, retreats, etc. I have also read countless books and articles and have browsed more websites for a variety of information than I could ever have imagined possible. Then there is the onslaught of YouTube videos and Ted Talks that I breeze through from time to time.

Many of you can identify.

I have found there are generally three things that happen:

1. Something is learned

2. Time has been wasted

3. I have been reminded of something I already knew but a new delivery has proved refreshing and beneficial.

As time goes on, it is point-3 that is the game changer.

Let me explain. Learning something new can be interesting and even inspiring. But when I am reminded of something that in the back of my mind I have known to be true, and which has stood the test of time and experience, I am often launched into action.

Now, change happens when I move from an agreeable thought to a practice or discipline. And if I attend an event or if I read or watch an informative piece of material and put even one thing I've found out into play, it has been worth my learning or re-learning effort.

I refer to this as The 1% Principle. A small but healthy habit can serve to propel me from stagnation into intentionality. The right bit of information put into practice at the right time can make all the difference in the world when it comes to finding energy to keep your dream alive.

If by the end of this book, you have brought even one thing to the point of a regular mindset and habit, you may find yourself not only rising to the challenge of life, but taking your dreams to the next level.

THE BIG PICTURE

Okay. You have looked at the cover of this book and read the subtitle that says, "finding energy to keep *your* dream alive."

There are a few things to say at this stage.

First, I emphasize *your* dream alive instead of *the* dream alive. There is the imposition of culture and media that *the* dream is the large salary with the big house and white picket fence with lots of toys and a happy family with which to enjoy them. Maybe this is your dream. But maybe it's not or maybe it's more than you dream. The bottom line is that it has to be *your* dream.

The next thing I'm about to say came as a bit of a surprise to me. When I have asked people what their dreams were I often got a blank stare. It seems many have never had a dream or else somewhere along the line, they've lost it.

Sad.

Life for these people has become more about maintenance and even survival than it is about having a dream worth chasing.

What do you think of the following statement?

"You are your dream."

This past New Year's Eve my wife and I had the privilege of hanging out with my daughters, their significant others, our two grandkids, and a number of my daughters and husbands' friends. This group included commercial real estate agents, lawyers, oil company managers, a not-for-profit specialist, a farmer, a social worker who also does photography, a nurse, a teacher, a voice-over professional, and a federal-government employee. As we were around the dining room table I asked the question, "Do you have a dream?"

The majority of these people went blank for a moment and then stated that they were living their dreams. They said that they enjoyed their work, loved their families, had reasonable health and wealth, and were basically content.

These people had become their dreams. That's not to say they still weren't working at building future plans, but each was now in a chapter of his or her life where a dream he or she had in the past was reality.

By saying, "You are your dream," I am saying that the way you think about your purpose, values, and future will determine what matters to you, what you "dream" about, and ultimately how you live each day.

HOWEVER...sometimes the problem is that our energy tanks are empty. We have run out of steam. There is nothing left to give. We aren't so much worried about our dreams as we are about finding the strength to keep on keeping on.

This is the purpose of FIYT (Fuel In Your Tank).

So whether you are just in need of a top-up or you have run out of fuel completely, this book is for you.

IN THE RING

1. What is one thing you have learned from a book, class, or conference that you have applied to your life?

2. Are you in the midst of living your dream, pursuing your dream, or trying to find a dream worth chasing? Explain.

3. Would you say your energy tank is full – that it's time to fuel up – or that you are running on fumes? Why have you given this answer?

4. Are you willing to learn or relearn a mindset or habit/discipline that might just fill up your energy tank and free you once again to dream-chase? Why or why not?

CHAPTER ONE

DREAMS

DAY DREAMING

I remember as a high school student spending time gazing out the window of the classroom and drifting into Never Never Land. It was a fun place to go because in that outer space of the mind I could create a planet where things were as I wanted.

For me, that usually involved playing in a rock band, traveling the world and having fun doing it. Now, I'm sure I was the only guy that ever had this dream...!

I picked up my first set of drumsticks when I was twelve. I really wanted to get a motorcycle, but my mom was terrified of what might happen to me.

So, my parents agreed to buy me drums and put me in lessons instead. At the age of fifteen, I began to join with other musicians a little older than I was and we began to practice covers such as "China Grove," "All Right Now," and of course, "Smoke on the Water." We would play in basements or garages and more often than not our listeners involved a few friends, tolerant parents, and annoyed neighbors. Eventually, we played in schools or pubs. And that was the direction I wanted my life to take. That was my dream.

I did play sports as well. High school football and city hockey leagues kept me active and provided for some great friendships. But that wasn't my dream. My sports were just a way of living life "in the meantime."

By the way, did you know that "in the meantime" is where we live most of our lives? We are always waiting for something. I am convinced that learning to live well "in the meantime" is a key to a fulfilling life.

After all, isn't it true that even when we accomplish a dream, we are soon on the lookout for the next one?

Anyway, back to my dream about becoming a rock star. As you might have guessed, it never happened. And I'm okay with that. However, I still play drums and on occasion throughout my life I have played in cover bands and had a blast doing it. No regrets.

As I became a young adult, my dreams shifted. I wanted to become a pastor in a church and help people. Go figure. From dreaming about playing in a rock band, to dreaming about getting a theological education where I could help people find their way to a life that involved loving God and others. I still can't completely figure that one out except for the fact that I had one of those praying moms who never quit praying for me to go into the ministry. You see, that was one of her dreams.

As a kid, I hated when my mom told me she was praying that I would be a pastor. That was about the very last thing I wanted to do. It sounded so boring and restrictive to me. Yuck!

I guess the joke was on me. I have spent the last thirty-four years of my life doing what I never, ever saw myself doing. I guess that speaks volumes about my mom's prayer life and a God who has a sense of humor. And here's the thing. I really do believe I have one of the best occupations ever. I assure you there has never been a dull moment.

My dreams didn't stop there. I wanted to marry a beautiful girl and have great kids. I wanted to have a nice car. Someday, I wanted to live in a place without snow. I wanted to travel to all kinds of places that I had never been to before. Enjoying sports and friendship were always ongoing dreams. Then there was another dream that seemed so far away. I wanted to see the Chicago Blackhawks play live and before I died, I wanted to see them win a Stanley Cup.

So, how did my "dreaming" turn out?

Well, I married a girl that I had met back when I was thirteen years old...and she was twelve.

She is gorgeous and has aged like a fine wine! I have two incredible daughters, who have exceeded my expectations on so many levels. I even have two grandkids who are perfect. Aren't all grandkids that way? I have usually had a nice car to drive (sometimes to my wife's dismay...not part of my dream!) I am currently living in Victoria, British Columbia where after three years I have only seen a week's snow in total. I have traveled to places like the Congo, Colombia, Uruguay, France, and many great places throughout Canada and the United States. My favorite of all places is Maui, which I have been to many times. In my fifties, I am still playing sports and enjoying some great friendships. AND...get this...I have been to Chicago to see the Blackhawks play and have celebrated three Stanley Cups in the last six years.

I am a fortunate man. I know that. In fact, I have said to my wife that if God took me home today I would die a happy and thankful human being.

But I haven't always felt this way. Along the path of pursuing my dreams, I got tired, grew discouraged, and wanted to give up. There were times when I wasn't sure if my wife and I would make it through some of the rough spots in our marriage. A couple years back, my wife was diagnosed with breast cancer. (Thankfully, she is now a cancer survivor.) We had some tough times with our daughters during which we seriously questioned our parenting skills. At times, having nice cars has caused some serious stress points in my relationship with my wife. Being in Victoria is great, but we miss our kids and grandkids back in Calgary. For many years, though I wanted to travel, I was deathly afraid of flying. I have had a few sports injuries that have restricted my ability to function at times. AND...I know this will really bring the tears...I had to wait till I was fifty to see the Hawks win the Cup!

All this is to say – dreams don't come easy. Especially certain dreams. There are dreams that I am still chasing and there are even dreams I have given up on.

However, I will never give up dreaming and somehow, some way finding a way to keep moving forward.

How about you? Do you have dreams you are trying to get a hold of?

Have you named them? Do you have a game plan? Have you prioritized your dreams? Or are you all worn out from the everyday mess of life, to the point of exhaustion and frustration?

The worst-case scenario is to quit and become discouraged, skeptical, and eventually cynical.

It could be that you need some help just as I do from time to time. I need a book, a friend, a conference, a counselor, or divine intervention to get me going again.

One of the most powerful two-word phrases is this: "DIE TRYING."

Did you get that? If you are still passing the mirror test (fog on the glass) it means you are still breathing and have a dream to go after.

There can be a few roadblocks in all of our lives that we need to think about. Keep in mind most roadblocks mean that there is a detour. In our path of life, the detour is usually up to us to discover.

Consider the following Roadblocks.

ROADBLOCK #1 - THE YOUNG FAMILY STAGE

As I look back, this was one on my favorite times in life. Watching our daughters grow up and having the privilege of being a part of their upbringing has been a dream lived out. I remember the basketball and volleyball games, the school plays, the family vacations, the Christmas celebrations, the birthdays, the church spring camps, the drives, the talks, the milestones, and on and on it went. We were (and still are) a close-knit family.

And in the midst of this, it seemed like family, occupations, and playing some hockey was about all there was time for. However, I learned that this was where many dreams were born. Every now and then those dreams could be chased but it was often a stop-and-start process.

A word of advice in this stage. Learn everything you can about dream chasing. I encourage journaling as a way to record lessons learned in the process of life. Most of us would say that a lot of learning has come through making mistakes. In fact, someone once told me to learn to embrace mistakes. Mistakes can be friends who save us time down the road.

My heart does go out to single parents. My youngest daughter is in this stage and it can be all-encompassing to say the least. If ever there was a time to live out the "it takes a village" saying, it's at this time. My daughter has family and friends who have come alongside of her to make life work. Alyssa and Paul, our oldest daughter and her husband, have been prime examples of selfless people who bring much help and joy to our young-est daughter and grandson, who is now seven years old.

In the midst of becoming a single parent at the age of nine-teen, our daughter, Arika, kept dreaming. One of those dreams included becoming a nurse. As a family we pulled together and over the next five years we became an integral part of Arika and grandson Josh's village. And in 2012, Arika graduated as an RN. She now works at the Tom Baker Cancer Center in Calgary, AB. AND this is her dream job.

By the way, never overlook family members as part of your "hero" list.

More about that later.

ROADBLOCK #2 - THE GOOD INCOME STAGE

How can a good income keep someone from chasing his or her dreams? Well, the answer is really quite simple!

Money can be a trap. Once we get accustomed to a certain level of income, we become convinced that we can't live on anything less. In fact, we build this false sense of security on the idea that money equals happiness. Ha! Haven't we learned over the centuries of human existence that money does not bring happiness? I am convinced that people with a lot of money lose more sleep at night about what they have and don't have than those with moderate incomes. In my limited travels to very poor areas of the globe, I have seen that people with just enough to get by seem happier and more fulfilled. That is a crazy revelation for those of us living in a wealthy country.

When I considered the move to Vancouver Island...the land of little to no snow...I knew that it meant a decrease in income. I was leaving a large church in an economically sound city like Calgary for a small church in an economically challenged place on the island. It meant a twenty-five percent decrease in salary and my wife would initially be unemployed. By the way, she had a great job with the federal government.

My friends and coworkers in Calgary never really thought I was serious. But I was. And let me tell you, I have not regretted the move for even a day. There have been a number of good things that have taken place on so many levels. This includes my wife being re-employed with the federal government in a job she loves.

I can't begin to tell you all the aspects I enjoy about living here...yes, including the mild winters. I believe that Vancouver Island is one of Canada's best-kept secrets.

And you? Are you stuck in the money trap at the cost of pursuing your dreams? Maybe it's time to take a calculated risk and go for the desire of your heart. At the end of the day, what good in life ever comes without some kind of risk?

ROADBLOCK #3 - THE RETIREMENT STAGE

The word "retirement" has this sense of end to it. For many it has become a time to sit and back enjoy all the good things they haven't had time to enjoy up to now...a dream in and of itself. Others would say that is in these final years that they can now really chase the dreams they have had for years.

One of the many advantages of my profession is that I get to see all stages of life...literally from the cradle to the grave. I encounter the rich and the poor, the healthy and the sick, those in marriages or partnerships, those who are single or single again, the happy and the sad, the smart and the not-so-smart, the retired, and those who wish they could retire. And one of the most inspiring things I have learned is that all of these stages or "states of being" have nothing to do with whether or not someone is a dream chaser. Dream chasing is not a "someday" event – it is an attitude to be chosen every day.

Oh, and don't wait to retire to pursue your dreams. Start now. Find a way. Find the energy. You do know that the idea of retirement is still a fairly new concept in modern civilization...right?

ROADBLOCK #4 - THE LAZY STAGE

At first glance, the perception of lazy is a picture of someone slouched on a couch, watching TV, and eating junk food. Chances are this person is making a living off of someone else and has zero drive. However, the face of lazy and the reasons for being lazy are varied.

The most common definition of lazy is "averse to work." Another often unmentioned part of the defining of lazy is "slow moving." Whatever the definition, it suggests that there isn't a lot of action or any results happening.

I have seen and personally learned that laziness is often covered in a swirl of activity. From the outside "lazy" could hardly be associated with such a fast-moving, busy, busy, busy type of life. But at the heart of all the noise is the fear of being discovered.

In my first summer job as a sixteen-year-old, I worked at a plant, making clay pipe. It was a hard-grind type of job, but it was a great workout and paid really well. It was here that I met a guy in his fifties, who always seemed to be doing "something." On the outside he seemed to be a go-getter...maybe even a dream chaser.

One day I had a chance to work with him, which proved to be one of life's more interesting lessons. He told me that the key to staying employed was to always "look" busy. As a newbie at the plant, I was sure a tried-and-true worker such as this man could teach me much. But to my surprise, he told me he had no idea how to do many tasks. He always avoided learning anything new because then there would be greater expectations! A year and a half later, I met this man on a cold winter evening in a parking lot. He was selling Christmas trees. He had been let go and was just trying make ends meet.

Okay, at least he was working. But he was lazy. And my guess is that underneath his laziness was a fear of failure. Maybe it was because of a father who'd told him he didn't have any worth, or because of some bad experiences in his education or early work years. But his life had taught him not to try too hard because nothing good ever came from it. Hmmm.

I tell this story because I believe that often...not always, but often...the lazy have had some bad raps and need someone to come alongside, help them understand their worth, and walk them through some successful endeavors. Being able to do this has been one of my dreams.

If you have been told you are lazy all your life, chances are that you have been more than willing to live up to those expectations. But deep inside you may have a dream or two worth chasing you. Don't give up. Don't resign yourself to the opinions of others. Somehow, some way, find the energy to chase your dreams.

ROADBLOCK #5 - THE CAREGIVER STAGE

Two words to consider: sacrifice and bitterness.

I admire those who take care of family and friends at a time when these people can't help themselves. This is a noble act and one that gets overlooked in what can be a selfish culture. May God bless you and give you daily strength in your efforts.

SACRIFICE comes when we choose to give of ourselves to help those in need. Sacrifice means we are giving something up. We are considering the needs of others before our own.

BITTERNESS comes when we forget to take care of ourselves and lose sight of our dreams. Dreams are a part of who we are. I recommend we continue to pursue our dreams even during these times in life. It can be in the smallest way. It could be reading, taking time to talk to a friend, or jotting down a few thoughts just before we bed down. Whatever it takes, keep your dreams alive. If you don't, you may find that you are wearing out to the point where you feel there is nothing left to give. And that spells disaster – not only for you but for the one you are caring for as well as other friends and family.

Keep your dreams alive and in doing so, you will find the energy you need to keep moving forward.

There is one other aspect of life that I want to address that affects our dream chasing. This is when crisis or tragedy strikes in our personal lives.

Listen up. There are times in life when it takes everything we have just to do the daily minimum. And that's okay. We all have difficult times. It is essential that we take "time outs" to mourn or grieve a major loss, get well when the body goes down, and reflect of life when meaningful relationships go south.

It's okay to push pause. But at some point, the movie needs to start again.

We now move on to get to the heart of FIYT CLUB. That is, to find ways to gain energy to chase our dreams.

IN THE RING

1. Which quote do you identify with the most and why?

"There is only one thing that makes a dream impossible to achieve: the fear of failure."

— Paulo Coelho, *The Alchemist*[1]

"Hold fast to dreams,
For if dreams die
Life is a broken-winged bird,
That cannot fly."

— Langston Hughes

The most pathetic person in the world is some one who has sight but no vision."

— Helen Keller

"Never, ever, let anyone tell you what you can and can't do. Prove the cynics wrong. Pity them for they have no imagination. The sky's the limit. Your sky. Your limit. Now. Let's dance."

— Tom Hiddleston

"Some people see things that are and ask, Why?
Some people dream of things that never were and ask, Why not?
Some people have to go to work and don't have time for all that."

— George Carlin

---

1 Coelho, Paulo. *The Alchemist*. Harper Collins. 1993. print

2. Again...are you in the midst of pursuing a dream, living out a dream, or in need of finding a dream worth chasing?

3. What has been your past experience in chasing dreams? What have you learned from your experience?

4. Who is a dream chaser you admire and what is it about that person that causes your admiration?

5. What might be a roadblock to your dreams? If there is a roadblock what is the best way to go about finding a detour?

CHAPTER TWO

THOUGHTS

SHIFTING GEARS

I love cars.

I don't love cars the same way I love my family, my friends, or even my dog. But I love cars in that there is something about getting behind the wheel of a fun-to-drive car that gets the heart pumping. In my life, I have had the privilege of driving and owning a few such cars.

I learned to drive on a 1973 Mazda RX-3. There was nothing overly special about. It was my dad's commuter car. It was light-blue in color and was a typical import of the day, which meant no bells or whistles.

However, what got my juices flowing when I drove this car is that it had a 4-speed standard transmission.

When I got behind the wheel and turned the key, I was about to enter a world I had been waiting for my whole young life. But before I could gain the benefit of racing around town in a car like this, I first had to master changing gears.

It was difficult at first. It would have been so much easier to learn on my mom's Cutlass with its automatic transmission. But my dad wanted me to learn on a stick shift. Good decision, Dad!

Now, changing gears took patience and co-ordination. There were times when I would pop the clutch too soon and stall the engine, or grind the gears because I hadn't pushed the clutch in far enough, inducing a cringe on my dad's face. But he and I both hung in there and before long, changing gears became a smooth process that changed a cringe into a smile. And once I mastered the shifting process, driving a standard was a blast.

Okay. So why am I talking about shifting gears when the theme of this book is "finding energy to chase our dreams"? Well, here is the reason. It's a critical one, so listen up.

IF I AM GOING TO FIND THE ENERGY TO CHASE MY DREAMS, THEN I NEED TO LEARN TO SHIFT THOUGHTS IN A SMOOTH AND ORDERLY WAY SO I DON'T STALL THE ENGINE OR GRIND THE GEARS.

Let me explain.

Throughout the course of any given day, we have many thoughts that come and go in our minds. This includes thoughts in regard to our jobs, our interactions with others, our responsibilities, thinking back, thinking ahead, decisions that need to be made, worries, planning, and so on and so forth.

When our minds overload, it can result in moments of brain stall. When our minds try to cover too many things, we brain grind. The challenge is to learn to shift gears from one subject to another in a smooth and orderly fashion. And if we learn to do this without stalling or grinding, we will be able to shift into overdrive gear at certain moments throughout the day where we can focus on our dreams.

It may be during a coffee or lunch break, a drive or walk, when we are getting ready in the morning, an hour of time for ourselves during a day off, or moments when we awake in the night. Instead of being stuck in a high-rev gear, we need to change to the overdrive, where we take a deep breath and let our minds go to the dreams we want to chase.

This may sound a bit foreign to you, but let me assure you that learning to shift our thoughts smoothly can be a game changer.

Here are four ways we can learn to be better gear changers.

1. **WALK** to release

Have you ever been stuck in a thought and unable to shift at all?

I'm sure you have. It can cause us to lose sleep, forget things we were supposed to do, and hold us hostage no matter how hard we try to shift.

One practice that has helped me from time to time is just to go for a walk. The scenery changes and if you put that together with a bit of physical exertion, shifting from one thought to another becomes easier. Taking a walk can provide a way for us to release or rather to become released from a sticky thought. This can provide new energy in our minds to move into a dream-chase moment.

My wife and I live in a beautiful environment. The area is called Bear Mountain, and it is a recreation and golf resort. It is also made up of residential communities. A drive or a walk throughout this development can assist in releasing stressful thoughts and provide the shift into dream mode.

Often I find myself in the downtown Victoria area as well. There is just something about the inner harbor and ocean that brings an automatic sigh of relief and frees the mind to explore life's options and go to the wonderland of dream chasing

Consider your own beautiful places in your community. Every place has them. And then determine that at least weekly, if not daily, you will explore and walk to release.

By the way, a dog who won't leave you alone until you get up and go for that walk never hurts. More about Tessa later.

2. **WATCH** to engage

When you watch a movie, what is the state of your mind?

What I mean is this. Do you watch a movie and let the mind just become sponge or do you intellectually interact with what you see and hear?

We all need to escape reality at times. However, I have found that every now and then there is a teachable moment that can fuel our dreams or at least provide some motivation in moving ahead. Two specific examples come to mind.

The first one is from the movie *The Untouchables* with Kevin Costner.

There is a part where Costner, as Eliot Ness, has just fouled up an attempted bootlegger bust. The newspaper is all over it and an article revealing his horrible mistake makes a mockery of him. In a powerful scene, Ness takes the clipping from the newspaper, pins it on his corkboard, and says, "I'm making so many mistakes, I'm beginning to enjoy them." In other words, he is not afraid of mistakes. Every one of them has taught him a lesson.

The second example is from another gangster movie called *The Departed* with Jack Nicholson. Nicholson's character, Frank Costello, makes a rather arrogant statement at one point, which does carry an element of truth for those who desire to see their dreams become a reality. He says, "I'm not a product of my environment, my environment is a product of me!"

There is a negative side to this statement in the context of a bad-guy gangster dude. But the positive side is that if we are to move forward in life, including in the chasing of our dreams, then we need to be leaders who are influencers...Just sayin'.

When we watch or listen or even read in an engaged way, there is so much that can be gained. There is so much that can help us make a gear change.

3. WEIGH to discern

How do you determine what will influence the way you think?

This question implies that we are capable of sifting through all our thoughts in such a way that we will be able to figure out which thoughts are worth keeping and which thoughts need to go in the recycle bin.

Yesterday my wife shared a great quote she'd read: "Don't be so open minded that your brain falls out." I have been guilty of being influenced by so many ideas and opinions that all it has done is cloud my thinking and jam the gears. When the gears are jammed, not only are we not able to dream chase, but we are in danger of giving it up altogether.

Here are a few tried and trusted ways we can put the thoughts and opinions of others on a scale to weigh their worth:

- Consider the source of the information you are processing. Is it reliable?

I confess that a lot of the information I get comes from Facebook. Even when it comes to hearing fast-breaking news, I often read about it in a post before I read, see, or hear about from the official media. This has bitten me in the butt at times; for instance when I bought into a post that promised me a free iPhone 6s...and yep...you guessed it...a virus worked its way through everything. Will I ever learn?!

- Determine whether or not the information is transferable to your situation. Will it work?

A good idea for someone else does not automatically mean it's a good idea for me. I have been doing research on whether to self-publish or to go the traditional route of getting an agent who has more connections to find a publisher. I am finding that what works for one person might not have necessarily worked for someone else. And even those who've had success with self-publishing have different opinions on how to go about it. So think through all the advice you are getting and save yourself energy that could be put to better use.

- Communicate these thoughts and opinions to trusted friends or mentors. What do they think?

I am fortunate to have great family, friends, and co-workers who are brilliant. Seriously. When I share my findings in regard to a dream I am pursuing, they are honest, forthright, and wise.

The most helpful person is my wife, Cheryl. I have never met a more analytical thinker in my life. She helps me ask all the right questions and challenges me to do better. She can be annoying at times (that's a secret between you and me by the way), but I am convinced that those who love us most will push us to become better. I don't know what I would do without those who surround me and are there to help me succeed.

- Project the expiry date of the information. Will it last?

Ideas that are good today may not be good ideas tomorrow.

I had a craving for chocolate milk. I checked the expiry date and was sure that I would finish it long before that date ever came. I had a few sips, right out of the carton, and then the next time I went for a sip, it had turned to chocolate sour cream. I guess I was wrong about my chocolate-milk drinking habits.

Much of our dream chasing happens over time. Make sure that when it comes time to implement an idea or thought, that it is still relevant. Again, another energy saver in the long haul.

- Try these ideas on for size. Do they fit with our values and beliefs?

Depending on what our dreams are, there may be times when we will have to make a decision about whether or not we'll compromise something that we hold as a value or belief.

Here's an example of what I mean. One of my dreams in living out here on the island was to get my motorcycle license. After achieving that in a relatively short period of time, I wanted a Harley Davidson. After much searching I found the one I wanted. I was in love! It was at this point that I had a decision to make. I had learned that in the province of British Columbia there was principal tax even on used vehicles. This had not been the case in Alberta where I had lived for the prior twenty-two years. Someone had told me to just ask the seller to write down a lower amount on the bill of sale and then the tax would be less and could save a few hundred dollars. For a moment there was a dilemma. But my value of honesty ruled the decision. It would have cost less but not really. A few hundred dollars was easier to pay than to feel like I had compromised my belief system. Sometimes great ideas have to be passed over for good reasons.

4. WRITE to process

I recently visited a ninety-one-year old lady in the hospital. A couple weeks earlier, her mind had been sharp and her humor was intact, though her body was failing. But on this day her mind was foggy at best. I have been her pastor for the past three years. She didn't know who I was and didn't even know where the church was that she had attended quite regularly. I know she has been fortunate to have her faculties for as long as she has had them, but it was still sad to see her memory failing. Thankfully she still had a sense of humor as she joked about the state of her mophead hair.

Now, I don't know about you, but my memory gets tested from time to time. My buddy Al and I have attended hockey games and for an entire period we rack our brains trying to remember players from the past who have had certain skills or statistics. When we can't remember, we laugh it off and eventually cheat and look it up on our cell phones.

We live in a time of information overload where we are lucky if we remember our own names. FYI, it has little to do with age. Therefore it is a necessity to make a record of our thoughts in whatever form works. I like to use the notes app on my cell for initial thoughts. Then I sit down with paper and pen and write, scratch, and try and make some kind of sense of the thoughts going through my mind. Later, I'll go to my tablet for a more organized plan.

When it comes to dream chasing I will gain energy as I discern some kind of order that is beyond random thoughts. When I am left to random thoughts I succumb to forgetfulness, frustration, and a lack of focus. My mind gets tired.

Ultimately, I write to remember. It keeps me from trying to recall that thought I had yesterday that seems so far away.

FINAL THOUGHTS...

I end this chapter by bringing up the automatic transmission and paddle shifters.

First, let's look at the automatic transmission. Why won't the automatic transmission-illustration work when it comes to our thoughts? The answer is straightforward. If we let our minds shift automatically, they will go to whatever is before us. The tyranny of the urgent will stop us from chasing our dreams. The day-to-day stuff will take over. We'll become slaves to whatever is before us and fail to be in control. And like driving a car with an automatic transmission, we'll just go with the flow to our own dream-chasing detriment.

Now, let's consider the paddle shifters. Why did they come into existence in the first place? Well, from what I can figure out, they put changing gears at our fingertips.

My Acura has paddle shifters. I enjoy them because I have the option of using the automatic transmission, or I can change the lever to "S" and go into the fun of paddle shifting.

However, I must say I really didn't understand the advantage of paddle shifting until I had the chance to drive a 700-horsepower Lamborghini Aventador around a race track at Exotic Racing just outside of Vegas. It was then that I appreciated the beauty of fingertip shifting. Wow. What a rush!

How can I incorporate paddle shifting into my thoughts? Here's the key:

Be intentional about what we allow in our thoughts, even including the background stuff.

Our culture is noisy. It seems almost impossible to be in a place where we are alone with our thoughts. Think about it (pun intended). Even when we are at home, we are quick to turn on the TV, put on music of some kind, or engage in a conversation. In our cars, either the radio or stereo is on. No matter where we are, we seem to be a culture addicted to our devices; such as our cells, tablets, laptops, or desktop computers. When we go out to a coffee shop, again...noise. And whether we realize it or not, this noise can be directing our thoughts into places we never intended on going.

So the key to incorporating the paddle shifters into our minds is simple. Learn to embrace the quiet and the still. Even learn to...hang on tight now...turn off our cells. You will be amazed how after a few deep breaths, settling down, and letting go of all the noisy stuff that distracts us from dream chasing, we will find ourselves in control of our thoughts like the fingertip touch of a paddle shifter. It will take some discipline and time but the result will astound you.

In 1985, I went to one of the most important conferences in my life.

John Maxwell was the presenter. To this day, I remember something he said about the way we think. It was this: "Your attitude determines your altitude." Our attitudes are nothing more than what we do with the thoughts in our heads. If we are going to find the energy to dream chase it is only logical that we learn to think right, so that in a proactive way, we can get closer our goals with a "never give up" mindset.

Of all the places you will go to seek the energy you need to be a dream chaser, your mind...the way you think...will always be #1. This is where it all begins.

IN THE RING

1. Which quote do you identify with the most and why? Which quote are you most drawn to and why?

"Whether you think you can, or you think you can't – you're right."

— Henry Ford

"The world as we have created it is a process of our thinking. It cannot be changed without changing our thinking."

— Albert Einstein

"All truly great thoughts are conceived while walking."

— Friedrich Nietzsche, *Twilight of the Idols*

"Simple can be harder than complex: You have to work hard to get your thinking clean to make it simple. But it's worth it in the end because once you get there, you can move mountains."

— Steve Jobs

"Every one who has taken a shower has had an idea. It's the person who gets out of the shower, dries off, and does something about it that makes a difference."

— Nolan Bushnell

2. Would you see yourself as a person who is a creative or a critical thinker? How are both important in dream chasing?

3. Are your thoughts helping you achieve your dreams or holding you back?

4. What helps you think progressive thoughts in regard to your dreams?; (i.e. books, movies, friends, music). Which of these help you shift gears in your thinking when you get stuck?

5. Do you find yourself thinking more about the past, present, or future?

6. Explain why you think this is true of you.

CHAPTER THREE

THE BODY

THREE-LEGGED RACE

I have the best dog ever. I'm sure if you are a dog lover, you would say you have or have had the best dog ever. Fair enough. However, there is something about my dog that makes Tessa unique.

She's a Yorkie. Some of you are saying, "That's not a real dog," and others are saying, "That's not a man's dog." I'm okay with your opinions. I get that.

But what makes my dog unique compared to most other dogs is that she only has three legs. She broke her front passenger-side leg not once, not twice but three times. No one told me that owning these dogs is like owning china dolls.

It all started when at only three months old she simply jumped off the couch. She let out a blood-curdling yelp and we knew it was major. The leg snapped like a twig. And we soon came to the realization we should have called her Money Pit. We took her to an emergency clinic on this given Sunday and they charged us $1000 to basically say, "Yep, it's broken."

To make a long story…the next year and a half involved two different tiny metal plates with as many as eight screws and many trips to the vet. Eventually, we had to make a choice: Take her to Vancouver for a $8,000-$10,000 surgery by an orthopedic surgeon, which had no guarantees; put her down (not for a nap); or have her leg removed. We chose the last.

By the way, a word of thanks to the great staff at Prevost Vet Clinic in Duncan, BC. They were amazing in all of this and did their best to keep the costs down.

Tessa adjusted easily. As a dog, there was no social stigma (though I could have sworn I saw a Chihuahua laughing at her one time), and the adjustment to a tri-pawed life was fairly smooth.

Here is an example of her adjustment. Earlier, I mentioned how I enjoy walks on Bear Mountain. From where we live, the incline is fairly steep. In the past, with four-legged Tessa, we would go up and down without any issues. Even with a splint covered in pink gauze she was capable of doing the walk. Now, not only did I have a Yorkie but a Yorkie with a pink leg. My female-friend ratio was increasing. Anyway, with three-legged Tessa we still did the walk. Only I carried her up the final steep part to our bench mark…which was actually a bench. I really didn't mind because I had wondered if we would ever be able to do this walk again.

Then came the day I will never forget. It was two weeks ago. We came to the point where I usually picked Tessa up, but she looked back at me with what I saw as a grin, and with her wagging, stumpy tail said, "I got this one!" She began running…seriously… running this three-legged race to our bench mark. And not only did she make it up, but she walked and ran all the way down as well. I confess I teared up. Tessa had taught me a valuable lesson:

Never let physical limitations stop you from achieving your goals, or in the case of this book, from dream chasing.

By the way, I haven't had to carry her since. Oh, and I bought her a Harley Davidson harness. She's now known as the toughest female, three-legged Yorkie on the mountain. The people in the cars driving by are always doing double takes. I'm so proud of her!

So...how does this relate to finding the energy to chase your dreams?

Well, it's simple. I sum it up in a phrase I use when I meet with couples for pre-marriage counseling. When it come our physical well being, "Do the best with what you got."

It's a paradox. When we spend physical energy to gain a healthy level of fitness, we will actually gain energy over the long haul.

I am going to "carefully" use a story from my wife, Cheryl. First, let me say she is the most amazing woman I have ever met. She is beautiful, intelligent, wise, and hard working. She is also a breast cancer survivor. And besides all this, she has put up with me for over thirty years. Crazy.

However, since moving out here to the island, she hasn't been as disciplined in her diet and workout regime. (You're getting the word "carefully" in all this, right?) Anyway, it wasn't so much that *I* was noticing a difference in her energy level and physical well-being, but it was beginning to get to her. She had no energy left at the end of her workday, and her clothes were beginning to feel uncomfortable. But then, she made up her mind, which is where it all begins, as I said in the last chapter, and she began to take control of her diet and fitness plan. In doing this, and here is the clincher, she has had more energy, is ready to go clothes shopping once again, and is back on track to pursuing her dreams.

I reiterate the paradox. When we spend physical energy to gain a healthy level of fitness, we will actually gain energy over the long haul.

I am going to introduce an acrostic to you that keeps this whole fitness thing as simple as possible.

The word is **MEW**...as in what a cat does. It stands for:

*M*ove and *E*at *W*ell.

At the end of the day, this pretty well sums up any decent fitness plan I have been a part of.

Let's begin with the **M**ove part. It can start by taking the stairs rather than the escalators, not always driving around endlessly trying to find the closest parking space to the door, or getting off the couch and doing a few chores around the house that have needed doing for a while now. Of course this isn't the only moving we need to do, but it begins to build a mindset that will lead us into the next level of discipline and sweat.

There are a few important "you don't have to" points to consider when finding a workout routine that fits:

1. You don't have to join a club to get fit. In reality, many join fitness centers for social interaction as much as for fitness reasons. I'm not against fitness clubs at all. It's just not a "must" if your goal is to get fit.

2. You don't have to buy expensive equipment to get fit. The majority of the fitness equipment I have purchased has been through online used sites. The equipment you find is often like new because people bought it new with good intentions but never got around to the workout part. The last equipment I bought, a recumbent bike, had been owned for a short period of time by a lady who had been in a car accident and was using it for rehab. It was like new.

3. You don't have to engage in workouts you hate in order to get fit. Find something you enjoy...at least for the most part. Many on the island enjoy walking, running, hiking, rowing or kayaking, biking or surfing. Vancouver Island is one of the only places in Canada where people can be involved in outdoor activities year-round without bundling up in layers of clothing.

4. You don't have to be alone to get fit. You don't have to be alone, unless you want to be. Those of us who are extroverts love being around people, and this is where being part of a gym or club will assist us. But again, I say it doesn't need to cost a lot of money. There is this site called "meet up" where people can join other small groups of people in a number of "moving" endeavors like running, hiking, or walking. Maybe a team sport like hockey or soccer is more your thing.

5. You don't have to have a personal trainer to get fit. However, I do recommend getting some good information from a reliable source. This will keep you from injury. Also, having someone to keep you accountable is never a bad idea when you are trying to get healthy.

I understand there are hardcore individuals out there who are incredibly fit, and for these people this is overly simple information. But the reality of our culture is that many are not where they want to be when it comes to fitness.

Personally, to stay somewhat in shape I have enjoyed a number of different activities. These have included hockey, squash, running, walking, dog walking (definitely different than just walking... dogs spend a lot of time stopping to sniff around), biking (stationary bikes and those bikes that actually take you places), light weight training, and I was even into skipping for awhile...with a rope, that is.

A huge part of health and fitness these days has become the Yoga phenomenon. My daughters enjoy it, a good number of acquaintances are engaged in it, and some have become yoga instructors. I confess to knowing little about this. So...all I will say is get informed and if it seems to fit, check it out.

The biggest problem most of us have to deal with is the cycle of initiative, preparation, a few valid attempts, and excuses why we can't do it two or three times, which turns into missing a few more times, which turns into discouragement, which turns into beating ourselves up. And beating ourselves up will not get us in shape.

The key word, as in everything, is discipline. By the way, did you know **discipline is our friend**? I know, some of you are convinced that discipline is more like that friend who keeps bugging you to get together and you keep making excuses why you can't meet up. It's time to get to know this friend...there is more to this friend than we are willing to admit.

Hear me on this. Getting fit will increase your energy to chase your dreams. *M*oving *AND* *E*ating *W*ell, that is.

One of my vices is eating out. It gets expensive and restaurant food is known to expand the waistline or love handles over time. However, this hasn't stopped me.

It goes back to when my wife and I were dating. Every Friday night we would go to a place in our home town of Regina called The Chimney. It was a great place for us to end the week and ease in to the weekend.

Eating out became a number-of-times-a-week thing. This became a habit we have hung on to. When our kids came along we just took them with us. They got to the point where they looked forward more to eating at home than going out.

Here in the Victoria area we have exceptional places to dine out.

Brown's Social House, Glo, 4 Mile Pub, and the Bard and Banker have been a few of our go-tos. Our favorite place is the Beagle on Cook Street (a must if you're visiting the area). It's a neighbor-hood pub with a warm environment, incredible food, and service second to none.

I almost forgot I am talking about eating well!

But here's the thing. It is possible to indulge every now and then and still eat well. Yep, every "now and then" I do the cheeseburger and fries. Many places offer healthier options. The truth is that I have been able to lose weight in the midst of the odd indulgence. The key is making good choices the rest of the time and to keep moving.

Another helpful suggestion is to share a meal. Cheryl and I do that all the time. A lot of places serve huge portions and will even double plate if you ask them to.

Many of my friends eat out often too. It has become an aspect of our culture. Part of the reason is our busy lifestyles. There is also the social aspect of eating out. It's nice to be out, to be waited on, to enjoy the atmosphere of the place, and not to have the mess to clean up afterwards.

Whether you eat out a lot or eat at home most of the time, it all comes down to being aware of what you are eating and how much you are eating.

Weight-loss diets can be great but usually aren't sustainable. A diet is helpful for those prepping to go on a holiday or getting comfortable for a major event. Some go on diets for health reasons – some for cleansing purposes.

In order for the *E*ating *W*ell part of *MEW* to work it has to be sustainable. This means eating food you enjoy in moderation.

Here is a timeless truth that will help us in eating well and pretty much every area of life that involves dream chasing:

EVERYTHING IS PERMISSIBLE

BUT NOT EVERYTHING

IS BENEFICIAL

Do you know where that's from? It's from the Bible of all places.

This suggests that I can do whatever I want...including eating whatever I want...but I would be wise to consider the results of my decisions down the road.

A challenge we have is that celebrating is almost always associated with food and drink intake. There are birthdays, going away parties, welcome parties, retirement parties, divorce parties, "I got a new cat" parties, "I just wanna" parties, etc. There are events such as weddings, anniversaries, celebrations of life, Thanksgiving, Easter, and perhaps the worst time of all is December. I was going to say Christmas, but we all know the eating and drinking associated with the holiday season goes far beyond one day.

So, what can we do to survive a December?

Well...plan ahead as much as possible. If ever there is a time when you don't want to mess up on your workout routine, it's now. When you go to a party or event, plan in advance to have one helping, limited snacks, and one or two drinks. For the lunchtime celebrations, eat a salad with dressing on the side so you are in control. When you eat at home, focus on fruits and vegetables and *a* chocolate – not a layer – from a box. You can still have a blast enjoying all the wonderful foods at this time of year without overdoing it. And January can be a month of maybe only having to lose two or three pounds instead of five to ten pounds, which as we all know is a big difference.

And once again, let's be reminded that **discipline is our friend**! What you do with your "friend," will determine your tomorrow. And your best friends will be the ones who bring out the best in you.

Regarding finding energy to chase your dreams and making sure your body becomes a source of that energy, there is an important question that needs to be asked:

When was the last time you saw your doctor for a physical?

I'm not talking about those times you have gone to a doctor because of that cold you couldn't get rid of, or that suspicious mole that you weren't sure you had seen before. I mean a full-blown, appointment-in-advance, complete, blood-testing, embarrassing-prod type of physical. Unfortunately, we often don't go, either because we are just too busy or we live with the "if it ain't broke, don't fix it" type of mentality. By the way, neither of those reasons are good.

I did my physical recently. There were no major issues. I did have a freckle checked out. I got some prescriptions filled. And I had a shoulder injury looked at. (I wish I could tell you that I injured my shoulder while chasing the puck into the corner of the rink – that me and another guy collided, and that as I was falling I was able to tip the puck over to the front of the net where a winning goal was scored. But I got it by chasing Tessa who had gotten out of the house and was about to make her escape. It was raining out, I was in my housecoat and slippers, I slipped on our drive-way, and down I went – ass over tea kettle. Meanwhile, Tessa stopped, looked at me, and ran to my wife who was at the front steps.) I thought I had separated my shoulder but I'd only torn a muscle, which was painful enough. Anyway, my doctor said things were showing signs of improvement and gave me exercises to do to keep it limber. Other than that, all was well.

The physical is critical to not only present-time well being, but also to future health. My wife was diagnosed with cancer during a standard mammogram. We remember the process clearly. The test, the detection, the biopsy, the subsequent meeting with the doctor to find out the lump was malignant, the surgery, the radiation, and finally, the six-month exams to show that she continues to be cancer-free. For us, it couldn't have gone any better. The doctors and health-care workers were amazing. And even the recovery went with very few hiccups.

This could have all been so much different if the cancer wasn't caught early through the check up.

So find yourself a good doctor if you don't have one already, and make regular appointments for your checkups. If our health goes south, at the very least our dream chasing will be put on hold for a while. And if this pause could have been avoided with a regular checkup, we will only have ourselves to blame. Avoid the pain of that scenario. If you are in need of a physical, start the process ASAP.

While we are talking about our physical well-being, I am going to take a moment to mention supplements.

Never before has there been such a flood of pills, liquids, nutrition bars, etc., which can be used to enhance our health and improve our energy. Please be careful. Many of us have a high trust factor based on what we find on the Internet but...hold on tight...sometimes sites provide false and even harmful information. Have a conversation with a specialist who is "in the know." And when you are in for your physical, tell your doctor about the supplements you are taking. He may nod in affirmation, but if you are taking something that is unhealthy or dangerous to your body, you are better off knowing.

And finally, a moment about overall grooming and style. You may be wondering what in the world that has to do with finding energy to chase your dreams. Well, more than you think.

I have mentioned my love of cars. Part of this affection involves constant detailing. You car people know what I'm talking about. A car that is stylish and clean and shiny just makes you feel better when you're driving it...really! In a similar way, when we take care of ourselves we tend to feel better about life in general. Feeling good about ourselves tends to fuel energy.

Remember what I said at the beginning of this chapter. DO THE BEST WITH WHAT YOU GOT. Maybe it's time for a makeover, some new clothes (which don't need to be expensive), a pedicure, manicure, or a new hairstyle. Even a massage can improve your posture by releasing stress.

Don't worry about measuring up to someone else or to someone else's expectations. Just do what feels right for you. Be proud of how God put you together. And then...work it!

To find the energy to chase your dreams, do yourself a favor by taking care of your body. There are no "trade-ins." What you have is what you got.

IN THE RING

1. Which quote do you identify with the most and why?

"Those who think they have not time for bodily exercise will sooner or later have to find time for illness."

 —Edward Stanley

"Fitness - if it came in a bottle, everybody would have a great body."

 —Cher

"I have to exercise in the morning before my brain figures out what I'm doing."

 —Marsha Doble

"If your dog is fat, you're not getting enough exercise."

 —Author Unknown

"There are really only two requirements when it comes to exercise. One is that you do it. The other is that you continue to do it."

 —*The New Glucose Revolution for Diabetes* by Jennie Brand-
 Miller, et al. rclay[2]

"I'm at the age where food has taken the place of sex in my life. In fact, I've just had a mirror put over my kitchen table."

 —Rodney DangerfieldWhat can be your worst excuse for not
 eating healthy?

---

2 Brand-Miller, Jennie, et al. *The New Glucose Revolution for Diabetes.* Da Capo Press. 2007

2. What is one thing you could begin to do that would improve your eating habits?

3. On a scale of 1-10, how are you doing with disciplined physical exercise? (1=hate this question! 10=excellent) Are you content with that number? If you wanted to up the number by one, what could you start doing this week?

4. How does physical health that you can control influence your overall energy?

CHAPTER FOUR

EMOTIONS

THAT FIRST CAR

The first car I owned was a 1972 Oldsmobile Cutlass S. It was red with white interior. It had a V8 350 rocket for a motor and ran like a dream. I put "meats and mags" (chrome Cragar SS wheels and wide tires) on it. The tires on the rear were so wide that I put air shocks in the back to provide the needed room. It was so tight that if someone was in the back seat the tires would rub. And the final touch was a Craig power play cassette stereo that came with the security feature of being able to pull out the entire deck and bring it into the house at night. This car was my baby.

I remember the day it came time to sell it. I was buying a Honda Prelude (talk about a change). I put a for-sale sign on it and advertised it in the newspaper. Within a few days a buyer showed up with cash in hand. My baby was about to leave my life forever.

This was an emotional experience that went beyond what I had expected. There were a lot of memories tied up in this car. It represented my high school years; my dating relationship with Cheryl; hanging out with my buddies; and cranking the tunes with windows rolled down, cruising Albert Street in my home town of Regina. I spent hours and hours washing and waxing my baby and went through bottles of ArmorAll keeping the tires jet-black to ensure the chrome of the wheels would pop out. When the buyer drove the car out of my driveway and went down the street I actually got choked up. And yes, it is the "car that got away." Car guys usually talk about that first car as being the car they still wish they had.

Emotion. Hmm.

Throughout our lives the influences on our emotions are massive. Our emotions can free us or paralyze us. They can lift us to new heights or imprison us in the darkest of dungeons. They can move us to accomplish great feats or they can push us to doing things that can hurt others and cause regret.

In other words, making sure we have control over our emotions, not they over us, is a must. Especially if they are to be part of the make up that will give us energy in chasing our dream.

Understand that control over our emotions doesn't mean shutting our emotions down. It means developing borders that will keep them from having devastating effects. It also means having a heart that can be opened to free healthy emotions so they can flow and nourish both ways.

Here are some ideas and practices that can help us keep our emotions as fuel for energy in our lives. Many of these are nothing new, but can be extremely helpful when put into play.

1. THINK FIRST

The majority of the stupid things I have said and done are because I failed to think before responding, or more accurately, "reacting."

I remember one experience when I was very upset after meeting a guy for lunch. The intent was just to get to know him better. He was one of our leaders and it was time to connect. During the meeting he was critical, abrupt, and offensive. As I was driving back from the meeting I was so upset that I decided to call him when I got back to my office and give him a piece of my mind. The call was made and there was a busy signal. Grace. Then I took a deep breath, let the air get to my brain, and I thought about it. You see, this fellow worked for a large oil company and was in charge of many decisions. I had chosen to meet him in the middle of his day. He was under stress and was in a mindset that involved his work, not a leisurely lunch with his pastor. I made the decision to let it go and move forward.

By the way, this was a great decision. This man wound up being a great board member and trusted friend. Go figure.

Thinking before thrusting ourselves into an emotional response can save us a lot of regrets. And we all know, regrets can hold us back from dream chasing and leave us empty. A THINK FIRST disposition can save us a lot of wasted time and energy.

2. TIME OUT

This is similar to the previous point, but very different at the same time. THINK FIRST has more to do with the everydayness of life and interactions. Taking a TIME OUT has more to do with the events and relationships of life as a whole.

I take a few TIME OUTs a year. This allows me time to do three things:

...look back

...consider the present

...and plan ahead.

Sometimes this involves a day and at other times I go away and take a few days. Above all else, these opportunities provide perspective.

Here is a good definition of perspective: it means "to put things into their correct place (and) make it clear for you and others (Urban Dictionary[3]). What a great "perspective" on perspective.

When events and relationships become messy and blurred it will take every morsel of energy in our bodies just to make it through the day. I'm sure most of you know exactly what that looks like.

About six or seven years ago, I took a day to be alone and think about my history and the family I was born into. Our birth family has a huge influence on who we are. From time to time it can be a healthy practice to try to gain some perspective in order to understand the past. We can make some realizations about the present and plan for the future based on our families' influence on us.

Anyway, on this particular day I embraced my birth order as the youngest child in my family. I also thought about the significance of an event I wasn't directly involved with, which nonetheless

---

3 http://www.urbandictionary.com/

had a huge impact on my upbringing. This event was the death of a sibling I never knew. She died at the age of eighteen months, a few years before my birth. I have two brothers (nine and eleven years older) who loved their younger sister and experienced the devastation it brought to the family as a whole.

OKAY...SO... this is where it gets a little strange. During this "time out" day I actually wept for a sister I never knew. Go figure. But somehow this was a moment of understanding some things about my upbringing. My mom lived with a broken heart and my dad mellowed considerably. Both of my brothers often told me how it was like my parents were not the same parents they had grown up with. At times my brothers saw me as the golden-haired boy who could do nothing wrong and got everything he wanted while they'd had really tough years. My dad was kinder than he had been before my sister's death, and my mom was extremely protective. I came to understand a whole lot about why some things were the way they were. This day I had taken for reflection became an emotionally healthy one, which freed me and helped me move forward. All because of a TIME OUT.

3. JOURNAL

Not everyone is into journaling. However, there is always benefit to having some kind of record of all that we have gone through and are currently processing.

I started journaling about twenty years ago. It was before journaling had become a fad. I would get up most mornings and write down what was going on in my life and a few of my thoughts and emotional reactions, and then I'd write out a short prayer asking God to help me in whatever chapter of life I was in. It was a discipline at first, but soon it became a part of my day that served to encourage and inspire me to keep pressing on.

I recall a time in my life where I was feeling empty and "stuck." I was doing the same things over and over again and was in a routine that seemed to go nowhere. I remember recording my thoughts, emotions, and prayers and some days felt as though God was ignoring me. Historically, writers have referred to this as the "dark night of the soul," (a phrase initially coined by sixteenth-century poet St. John of the cross).

Then suddenly, one unforgettable day, I had an open-eyed vision. Seriously. I'd never had anything like it before, nor have I had anything like it since. It was an image of being caught in a burning house and I felt as though I was going to die. This experience described exactly how I was feeling at the time. To move this story ahead, the vision progressed over a period of months and eventually I was able to experience a new kind of freedom and hope.

I tell you this to say it was journaling that helped me process the meaning of this "open eyed" vision and served to assist me in bringing meaning to this scary and yet exciting time in my life.

Please hear me when I say journaling certainly doesn't need to happen every day. But over time, if done even on a semi-regular basis, it can help to bring our emotional energy to a place where it can do the most good.

4. IDENTIFY

What is it that brings out the best emotions in you and what is it that brings out the worst emotions in you?

This is a bit of a trick question. It's a common one that can leave us scratching our heads or create a cause-and-effect mindset. In other words, we excuse ourselves from being in the driver's seat of our own emotional state due to some outside force or event.

Here are a couple of examples:

The other day I was driving into Victoria from our home, which is located about a half-hour out. It was the typical crawl that occurs over the morning rush hour. Usually every one gets in line and merges on to the main road in a fairly orderly fashion. Every now and then, somebody decides they will try and get ahead by driving past the merge lines and squeezing in one or two car lengths ahead. I'm really not sure why, but for some reason it ticks me off (nice version). Not in an angry, fist-shaking way, but more in a head-shaking, hands-in-the-air kind of way. It really shouldn't bother me. It's just traffic and people will be people. Isn't it strange how traffic has the potential to bring out the worst in us? When I was growing up, I witnessed my dad getting into a fist-fight over a parking spot. Strange.

Then there are those things that bring out the best emotions in us. Things like Skyping with my grandkids, Josh (7) and Avery (coming up to 1). When I see them...via video; pictures; or best-case scenario, in person, my emotional world rises to a new level of happiness. I am smiling just thinking about them.

Here's the lesson. When we IDENTIFY the triggers that induce emotional responses and learn to anticipate them, we can use them to our advantage. This can increase the mileage of our emotional tanks.

5. LEARN THE DIFFERENCE

Something else to consider and learn about when it comes to emotions is to determine which ones are helpful and which ones can be potentially harmful. There can be a fine line between these.

For instance:

...Caution and Fear.
  Caution will help us move forward with care.
  Fear has the ability to paralyze us.

...Concern and Control.
  Concern is healthy and can lead us in assisting others.
  Control is unhealthy and makes other people
  feel smothered.

...Love and Lust
  Love is all about others.
  Lust is all about me.

...Constructive Anger and Destructive Anger
  Constructive Anger is action-based and makes things better.
  Destructive Anger is reactive and causes destruction.

...Sadness and Depression
  Sadness is a natural outcome and is relegated to a period of
  time.
  Depression is complicated and is a state that can consume.

...Stress and Anxiety

Stress can be controlled.

Anxiety controls us.

...Sympathy and Empathy

Sympathy is feeling for someone...like "poor you.".

Empathy is feeling with someone...like "I feel your pain.".

These are a few examples of emotions that are close and yet distant at the same time. Learning the difference comes with experience, counsel, and learning from good books. Knowing and identifying these emotions within us can be the difference between allowing our emotions to build us up or tear us down. And of course, our emotions will have an influence on others as well.

6. EMPTY THE WHEEL BARROW!

Here's what I mean. No doubt there are people in your life that come to you and dump. You know. They have more problems and complaints than they know what to do with and they have chosen you to be the recipient of all that's not right.

I have (crassly) put it this way. It's like I am pushing my own wheelbarrow down the road, and someone comes and decides they are going to...ahem...take a dump in my wheelbarrow. When they are finished they move on feeling somewhat relieved, while I am left with the stench. When this happens again and again, it can cause extra emotional stress and even anxiety. Somehow I need to find a way to deal with this not-so-pretty picture.

Now, we should be kind to those who relieve themselves in our wheelbarrows because chances are that we dump into someone else's. Even so, somehow we need to find a way to "empty the wheelbarrow."

Here are a FEW suggestions:

... As soon as they leave, find a way to symbolically empty the wheelbarrow. A counselor friend of mine finds hand washing effective.

... If you pray, pray for them and leave all their "stuff" in God's hands. And move on guilt-free.

... Take their "stuff" in your wheelbarrow this one time, but point them in the direction of someone who may actually be able to help them with their problems.

...If he or she is a friend and has a tendency to "dump and go" in your wheelbarrow, let this person know you have enough in your wheelbarrow right now and would rather just do something together like go to a movie or talk about unrelated matters...Yep...we call that small talk. But there are times when small talk is a really good thing.

... Just say no. You are hopefully learning your emotional limits and need to build a fence with a gate around your relation-ship, whereby you are in control of what comes in and what goes out. This may be really hard for you because you don't want to hurt someone's feelings, but in some situations, for your own emotional health, you need stop people before they "dump."

7. UH, WHAT'S UP DOC?

Confession time. Throughout my life I have wrestled with anxiety and often have been pinned to the mat. It hasn't been pretty for my own well-being and certainly has had negative effects in the lives of others. And as we know, can wound those people we love the most.

Here are some of the symptoms I struggled with in wrestling with anxiety: over-reacting, obsessive worry, trying to control circumstances, trying to control others, heavy blinking, a tense body, lack of sleep, a short fuse, inability to concentrate on what others were saying, lack of perspective, lack of faith, closed hands, a hard head and a closed heart, and so on. Not pretty.

When we moved out to the island, my hope was that my anxiety would cease. Instead, it initially got worse. At first, there was less activity to focus on and fewer people to be involved with, but the result was more time to be anxious.

Finally my patient wife had seen enough and said, "You need to talk to a doctor."

I didn't like hearing that, but I knew she was right. It wasn't time to be stubborn. It was time to put on my big-boy pants and do as she had suggested.

We didn't have a doctor out here as of yet, so I was left going to a walk-in clinic. I prayed I would see someone who could help. My prayer was answered.

The doctor was a thirty-something female who related well and seemed to understand exactly what I was talking about. She asked the right questions. She asked me if there was any major event that was causing this current stress. I mentioned a few things, but she didn't let me off the hook. Then came the questions about how I was handling the stress. Her head-nodding responses affirmed I was doing the right things. She kept on and asked if I was seeing a counselor. I told her I had a great counselor, who I had been (and still am) seeing back in Calgary. Then she recommended a book, which I purchased that day, and it proved to be helpful.

She had me return for a subsequent appointment and only then did she recommend medication. I had tried everything up to this point with limited success, so I figured why not give it a try.

These meds were a game changer.

Over the next few months, life looked and felt different. For the first time in a long time, my emotional life was fueling me instead of draining me. I was also able to be way more patient, present, and loving towards others. And I now had the energy to chase my dreams.

Go figure!

I am so thankful God created us with emotions. They are beautiful at best and can be brutal at their worst. We all know how unchecked emotions will lead us on a roller coaster ride that may be fun for a while but can wind up being hell on earth. Imagine being on even the most fun roller coaster. Now also imagine that the roller coaster operator goes for a break and doesn't come back. Still having fun? You get the point, I'm sure.

A number of years ago, I sat with two of our staff members from the first church I served in during my time in Calgary. I asked them this question: "If you had the choice between emotional pain and being numb, which would you choose?"

They both said they would take the pain, stating that it is emotion that makes us feel alive.

So true. Let's just do our best to oversee our emotions so they don't damage us or others. Let's understand and wisely rule over them, in order to build a healthy passion within us to chase our dreams.

IN THE RING

1. Which quote do you identify with the most and why?

"If you don't manage your emotions, then your emotions will manage you."

—Doc Childre and Deborah Rozman, *Transforming Anxiety*[4]

"When dealing with people, remember you are not dealing with creatures of logic, but creatures of emotion."

—Dale Carnegie

"The walls we build around us to keep sadness out also keep out the joy."

—Jim Rohn

"Be happy with others. Be sad alone."

—Unknown

"The finest emotion of which we are capable is the mystic emotion."

—Albert Einstein

---

4 Childre, Doc and Deborah Rozman. *Transforming Anxiety.* New Harbinger Publications. 2006

2. How do you usually manage your worst emotions such as fear, anger, and guilt? How could you improve this management?

3. What brings out the best emotions in you, and how in control are you of whatever that is?

4. Do you consider yourself an emotional person? Would the people closest to you agree?

5. What emotions give you the most energy? What emotions drain you?

6. Over the past month which has been more dominant, and how are you responding?

7. Is it time to talk to someone about "out of control" emotions? Who would that person be?

CHAPTER FIVE

RELATIONSHIPS

ROAD TRIP

Have you ever gone on a road trip? Did you enjoy it?

By the way, here is the definition of a road trip according to me:

A road trip is that event whereby two or more people travel from point A to some other point (!) and discover that the process of getting to wherever they are going is secondary to their destination. In other words, it's about the adventure of the trip with our travel companions.

Think right now of a favorite road trip experience. Does it make you smile, cringe, shake your head...or all of those...?

As I grew up, going on vacations with my family involved long driving trips with my dad at the wheel. He was a determined, pedal-to-the-metal kind of guy who had dangerous habits like passing when oncoming cars would have to either move over or hit us head on...Thankfully, they moved over. For him, it was all about getting from point A to B. Those of us in the car hung on for dear life. And when we had to pee, we were told to hold it, which we did until we were about to explode. Then when it was finally time to get out and go, it was like we were training for an Olympic "how quick can you go to the bathroom" event. These were not road trips I recall as pleasant memories. They were more like endurance tests.

The first road trip I can recall that was worth remembering, took place when I was sixteen. A couple of my friends and I were going to take a few days and drive from Regina to Edmonton. This was about an eight-hour journey. My friend Darwin was able to get his mom's Valiant. The Valiant wasn't fast or luxurious, but it didn't matter. It was all about getting away from real life and hanging out as friends and experiencing the freedom of the road.

Through my high school years, we did this a few times. None of the trips looked the same. The destinations were side notes. Our accommodations were cheap motels. And one time we slept in the car after being kicked out of our motel (long story... thanks, Scott...).

The main thing about the road trip was being with friends. It was about doing and experiencing life as it happened.

The energy or fuel that comes from good relationships through the road trip of life is critical to chasing and accomplishing our dreams. This may just be the most important way of gaining energy. I know it is for me.

Think for a moment about your past...include family members, friends as you were growing up, co-workers and bosses, coaches, trainers, people you dated, enemies, mentors...and the list can go on. Consider how these people influenced your thoughts. Think about how they made you feel about yourself. Now, understand how these people helped shaped your worldview. Acknowledge that they impacted your life...some for good and some for bad... whether you wanted them to or not.

Consider the present. Using some of the same groups as above, think about the people in your life. Who are the helpers? Who are the cheerleaders? Who is helping you achieve your goals and dreams? Who are the toxins? Who is putting pressure on you in a stressful way...or maybe in a helpful way? Who are you listening to? Who is "there" for you, but you are not listening to him or her? Who do you need to spend more time with? Who do you need to spend less time with?

All these questions and answers will help you build a future where you can gain a good, healthy mix of people in your life.

Know this: There are some relationships you can leave behind and some that you will have by necessity. And then there are those relationships that you desire, which will take time to cultivate. Be careful. Think things through. Make wise decisions.

I have developed a relational plan when it comes to developing healthy relationships. I call it the 5S APPROACH TO RELATIONSHIPS.

Here it is:

S #1 - SOLITUDE

SOLITUDE is about being alone. It's about finding sacred space.

Now, there is a big difference between being lonely and being alone. There is also a big difference between being alone and worrying about things and being alone in a position of peace. Solitude is the latter in both cases.

You may be asking, "What does solitude have to do with relationships?" I say everything. It is the difference between having healthy or toxic relationships.

When I choose to be alone I will find I am finally alone with my thoughts. And this can lead to asking good questions about relationships in my life.

Such as...

...who is lifting me up these days?

...who is tearing me down?

...are there people trying to control me?

...am I standing up against others when they are abusive toward me?

...am I expressing gratitude to those who love and care for me?

...am I being a good friend?

...are there things I need to say to someone or are there things I need to keep more to myself?

...who do I trust...who don't I trust?

...what relationships do I need to grow? Which ones might I need to end?

Imagine spending time alone and actually figuring these questions out. The answers may surprise us in some cases and incite us to action that at the end of the day will lead to better relationships. And remember what I said at the beginning of this chapter: "Relationships influence my life more than any other factor."

Solitude can also lead to interesting conversations with God. It is during those "alone" moments that you can express everything from thanksgiving to blame and anger.

Here's the thing. If God knows all things, he also knows our thoughts. There is no point in saying words that are nothing more than a lie. If this is something you do, be honest with God.

Also be honest with yourself. Did you know the person one can most often lie to is oneself? Think about it. My findings are that most of my problems and pains in life are things I have brought on myself and not the doing of others. I am guilty of lying to myself when I dodge the personal responsibility of my choices.

I have made solitude sound like it could be painful! It might be at first. It's just that we need to quit playing games within so that we can truly enjoy our times alone with a clear conscience. Sometimes we fear being alone because of inner issues we refuse to wrestle with.

At the end of the day, if I am at peace within and with God, solitude is beautiful and refreshing. It can stimulate new thoughts for our dreams and provide much rest that will fill our tanks in a whole new way.

A spiritual friendship is a relationship unlike any other. It is a relationship of integrity that provides mutual benefits such as trust, honesty, and consideration. It is a relationship that helps us grow to reach the potential we have and will assist our dream chasing. Potentially, the person in this relationship with you will be your biggest fan.

I have been fortunate to have a number of these types of friends over different periods of my life. One such friend I have known for just about twenty-five years now. We share common interests (cars, hockey, music, good lunch spots, etc.) but more importantly, we rely on each other to be there through the good and the bad times. We speak words of wisdom into each other's lives in a timely fashion. We lived in the same city for the vast majority of our friendship, but now live a good distance away from each other. However, we manage to connect on a regular basis through calls, texts, or in person. When we have something major happening in our lives, we automatically connect and dialogue. A lot of our friendship has been about keeping each other on track, or helping one another get back on track.

A spiritual friend may be a best friend but not necessarily. Sometimes best friends just do a lot together but never really go deep. And that's okay. They agree to stay away from certain topics, and that keeps them best friends.

A spiritual friend is not necessarily a soul mate either. In fact, many who have been spiritual friends to me are very different in personality, background, and interests. We don't do a lot together, but when it comes to being a valued voice, they are there, no matter what.

The following are some key qualities in a SPIRITUAL FRIENDSHIPS:

- Honesty

- Knowledge in life experience

- Trustworthiness

- Wisdom

- Reasonable Availability

- Transparency

- Caring

- Good Listening Skills

- Emotional Stability (for the most part!)

- Not Afraid to Confront Us

- Not Afraid of Silence

Now, here are some further thoughts on this subject...

- Many include your spouse/partner but not always.

- Rarely, if ever, call this person your spiritual friend!! It is a label that is okay to keep it to yourself.!

- Don't take this person for granted. It could be he or she lookslook to you for help as much as you look to him or her.

- Be forgiving as your SPIRITUAL FRIEND isn't perfect and may let you down on occasion.

- If you find out this person is sharing your thoughts with others...RUN!

Here are some hints in finding and keeping a SPIRITUAL FRIEND:

- Acknowledge the need for such a person

- Be patient

- Have a wide-angle view of possibilities

- Share carefully, especially in the beginning

- Avoid being "needy." That scares people away.

- Accept that a SPIRITUAL FRIEND may not be a forever friend. Hold on loosely. Refuse the temptation to control by guilt.

- Allow for "breathing" times in the relationship. There are times when there will be some emotional distance, which is normal. If you don't panic, the relationship will become close once again. You will pick up right where you left off.

S #3 - SMALL GROUPS

A small group is friends who do life together. You may find them in a local coffee shop, a neighborhood bar/pub, in a living room in a house, in a kitchen over coffee, doing a sport or hobby together, or in many other venues.

A small group provides the opportunity to discuss everything from current events to family dynamics. These people can serve to help identify who you are in the social structure of life. Maybe you are the introvert who enjoys people, but is quickly worn out from interactions. Perhaps you are the comedian who can make others laugh and lighten-up. Maybe you are the one who is always coming up with interesting facts or questions to stimulate discussion. It could be you are the facilitator who ensures that everyone is included. Perhaps you are the leader who has the greatest influence on the group. Whatever the finding, the small group is of great benefit to one's self-image, well-being, and ability to chase dreams.

In a case where you may be relocating, understand that it may take awhile before you the find the small group best suited to you. Therefore, experiment in a variety of settings to figure out where you belong. Don't feel bad about moving on if you need to. Find a place where "everybody knows your name"..and where you know their names as well.

S #4 - SANCTUARY

When many people think of a sanctuary, they think of a place in which to meet with God and/or to regain a sense of peace and perspective. Often the picture that comes to mind is that of a person being in a large, older style, majestic church. Sometimes this image involves a next-to-empty church, where there is plenty of space.

This is not my tradition when I think of church or sanctuary. To me a sanctuary is a place that is more a gathering place filled with music, voices, and often open expressions of emotion. It is a place where we can identify with other members of the human race and remember we are not alone. Sanctuary provides a sense of belonging to something bigger than just my own world. It brings a sense of excitement. It brings a sense of wholeness. It brings a place of safety.

This is the kind of SANCTUARY experience to which I am referring.

Now understand, I am referring to sanctuary in a symbolic sense. I am not just referring to church. I am referring to any place where a large group will gather for a common purposes that feed a sense of commonality. It may be church for you, but it may also be a concert, a seminar or conference, a sporting event, or a rally of some kind. It can even be a movie theatre, a theatrical production, or a show in Las Vegas.

I enjoy concerts and sporting events. I grew up going to Van Halen, Ted Nugent, Kiss, Supertramp, and so many other rock acts. I have always enjoyed sporting events...especially hockey. I have seen NFL and MLB games, but there is just something about the energy of a closely played NHL game...especially if my favorite team, the Chicago Blackhawks is playing. Watching them in Chicago was euphoric!

Sure, we can watch concerts, sporting events, movies, and conferences on TV, but there is just something about doing this with a larger group of people. It makes us feel a part of something bigger than ourselves.

And this is SANCTUARY. We do ourselves a favor by being a part of such a "ritual," if you will. It is dramatically different, than the Solitude, Spiritual Friendship, Small Group experience.

It is a stand-alone event that can lift us to a whole new level of dreaming and dream chasing.

S #5 - SERVE RELATIONSHIPS

Until recently, I used to speak about the 4S APPROACH to relationships. But I have added a 5th S. I call it SERVE.

The previous 4Ss are generally "all about me." But this S is primarily about others. It's about giving to others and serving alongside of others. And somehow this S brings all the other Ss together.

A good part of my life I have been inspired by others who have faithfully given of themselves to better others. This can involve everything from supplying a meal to a family or individual going through a difficult time, to a mechanic helping a low-income single parent with auto repairs and maintenance, to volunteering at a hospital or hospice, to helping take care of children in need, to loving on seniors in their time of need, to going to others' countries with a team to help with a variety of needs overseas.

And here is the observation I have made about those who SERVE on a regular basis: They seem to be more happy and content than those of us who live just for our own benefit.

This state of happiness and contentment is not the motivating factor for these people who SERVE, but it is definitely a byproduct. It just happens. I kind of think this is how God created us. When we help others, it brings us those inward feelings of worth we need the most.

AND NOW, FOR SOMETHING COMPLETELY DIFFERENT!

"REVIEW, REFLECT, RELEASE, REPURPOSE"

Time to be intentional. Some of the questions are repetitive, but this is meant to be an exercise. Remember, relationships are a huge part of finding energy to chase your dreams.

REVIEW: Take a tally of who is in your life and how those relationships are playing out. Use one word descriptions such as "great," "boring," "dead-end street," "intriguing," "healthy," supportive," "toxic," "fun," "encouraging," "burden," "abusive," etc. Those one-word descriptions will tell you a lot about what needs to be done.

REFLECT: Solitude can be a huge help on this one. Take time to understand why you have used the word you did to describe the relationship. Determine your contribution...good or bad.

RELEASE: There may be relationships that are in need of a "letting go."

Maybe it's time to stop trying to control another person and just let him or her be. Or, maybe this step involves letting someone off the hook. Maybe it's time to drop the grudge and move on...whatever that may look like.

REPURPOSE: In some instances, we may need to change the way we look at someone. For instance, there comes a time when a parent has to stop looking at their twenty-year-old like he or she is sixteen. The relationship shouldn't end, the role simply needs to be adjusted. Likewise, there comes a time when sons or daughters have to see their parents not as pro-tectors or providers or even authority figures, and begin to realize that it is time to give some TLC back to them. It is a beautiful sight when an adult child takes time to love and care for an aging parent.

I sincerely hope you have relationships in your life that are fueling your dream chasing. And that in turn, you are fueling someone else in the pursuit of his or her dream.

IN THE RING

1. Which quote do you identify with the most and why?

"Assumptions are the termites of relationships."

   —Henry Winkler

"Value your relationships, not your possessions."

   —Anthony J. D'Angel

"We can improve our relationships with others by leaps and bounds if we become encouragers instead of critics."

   —Joyce Meyer

"In a relationship you have to open yourself up."

   —Neil LaBute

"It is only when we no longer compulsively need someone that we can have a real relationship with them."

   —Anthony Storr

2. What is the most comfortable and uncomfortable part of being alone for you?

3. In your opinion, what makes two people best friends?

4. In a group of friends, what is your role: i.e. facilitator, listener, comedian, story teller, opinion giver, other? Are you content with your role? If not, how would you go about changing it?

5. Are you spending time with people who give you energy? If not, why not? Maybe you will find some of these people by serving others.

CHAPTER SIX

MONEY

BIRTHDAY CAKE

As I was growing up, it was tradition that we as a family would always celebrate birthdays together. What was really strange about this tradition was that the person who was having the birthday had to host.

Being the youngest in the family by a substantial amount, this usually meant all I had to do was show up. My mom would do the work and I just got to eat and open presents. Not a bad deal at all.

When it came time for birthday cake, we all knew that a quarter, dime, or a nickel would be in each piece. Sometimes they were wrapped in wax paper...sometimes not (a few germs were spread needless to say).

No matter whose birthday it was, I usually ended up with all the change, which wound up being a buck or so. That just meant a bit of extra candy that week, which was fine with me and the dentist.

I confess I have never been much of a saver. Truly, within days of my getting the birthday change, the money was all spent at the corner store on licorice, gum, pop, chips, etc. I have never had a shortage of ideas when it comes to things I could spend money on.

Thankfully, I married up. This is true on so many levels. And finances happen to be one of her specialties. Whew! Good thing.

I'm not so sure that good financial management is a key in finding energy to chase my dreams, but one thing I know for sure. Without good financing the headaches and stress of debt can create a vacuum of any kind of real creativity.

Following are some things I have learned and some things I am still in the process of learning when it comes to money. Take them to the bank.

This statement will be the basis of the things I have learned:

MONEY MATTERS, BUT IT ISN'T EVERYTHING.

Okay, so let's begin with the fact that one of the toughest challenges in life is balance.

Somehow we seem to swing from one extreme to the other.

I had a friend who was working through his view on speed limits. At one point, to the frustration of those lined up behind him on the highway, he would not go any faster than what the speed limit was. He was an obey-the-law kinda guy. But then came the day when he decided to buy a BMW M Roadster. Things changed. We did a road trip in the cool spring weather of Alberta, with the top down and heat on, going way past the posted speed limit. It was from one extreme to the other.

For many, this is how they deal with finances. Either it is a "to the dollar" budget...and not one cent over, OR they can go to the other end of the scale of taking the credit cards to the max... and then some. Both extremes can inhibit or destroy financial freedom.

By the way, here is how I define financial freedom:

"To live a lifestyle within my income that pays my bills, enables me to save even a small amount every month, provides for my needs and some of my wants, and allows me to be generous to others."

Let me break this down.

"To live a lifestyle within my income."

If I want to do a grandiose vacation every year; drive my dream car; live in a mansion; and wear only designer clothes BUT am making only enough to mooch off relatives on vacation; take public transportation because I can't afford a car (or motor scooter); live with my parents (or kids!...happening more often these days); and have been wearing the same sweatshirt for three years...then chances are I need to downsize my wants. Either that, or win the lottery. Maybe you think that "one day" that will happen. Hmmm. Think again. Figure out what this lifestyle looks like with your current income. Chances are some changes may need to be made, one way or another.

"That pays my bills."

Yep. It is a necessity to pay bills if I am going to be on a healthy path financially. It's quite funny how many overlook this fact. Now this is okay if you want to lose friends and go the bankruptcy route. But financial stability may take time as I pay what is owed and work hard doing it. By the way, do not bypass this step. It is crucial as you move ahead.

"Enables me to save even a small amount every month."

There was one occasion when I was a kid where I would do this. I saved my allowance and birthday money in a bank account so I could go to the fair every summer (bit of a carny at heart...).

My first debt came with my sixteenth birthday. You got it...a car. I bought it from my mom – the '72 Cutlass I mentioned earlier. She sold it to me for $800 (a steal) and I paid it off by working at the clay-pipe plant over the summer. The next summer, I worked the same job to pay off the Cragar SS wheels and wide tires I put on it...again through a family loan which was interest-free.

And then came the more expensive wants, when a bank that charged interest was involved, and there was a payment schedule over years, not months. (Yep...a car again.)

I was being drawn in to the "Why wait when you can have it now?" approach to finances. The problem with this was that my bills were always paid but what was left over was only enough for daily spending. I wish I had saved more. (Don't most of us?) However, I came across a saying that is changing things for me. "The best time to plant a tree is twenty-five years ago. The second best time is today."

Start saving something today. It will help out down the road.

A friend who serves in a pub, began to save toonies (two-dollar coins for those outside of Canada) over a period of months. Before long she had saved $800. This fund was used to help buy her daughter her grad dress. How cool is that! Get the idea?

"Provides for my needs and some of my wants."

There is a big difference between these two.

A NEED includes things like food (not junk food), shelter (not a house that has rooms I will never use), and usually in our day, some form of transportation (not a Ferrari..well maybe...)... and not a huge truck that uses tons of gas, never goes off-road, and is "too new" to haul stuff in. Anyway, you know what a need is.

A WANT on the other hand is very different. And the problem isn't with having wants, it's with deciding which wants need to be delayed for the sake of other wants that may play a part in the bigger picture of life. For instance, if you have a family to consider, maybe that vacation that can benefit everyone needs to take precedence over the upgraded vehicle. I did say "maybe." That's up to you.

"And allows me to be generous to others."

Here's a dangerous question to ask ourselves: "Do others see me as a generous person...or more of a tight and greedy person?" I think the answer to this question matters. It matters because it has a lot to do with my character.

Be careful. There is a "generosity" that is just for show in front of certain people. I'm not talking about that. I am talking about a generosity that benefits others. It might be a show of appreciation or love or simple kindness. But it reveals a lot about who we are.

A word about tipping. Both my daughters worked in restaurants as servers during their school years. They made minimum wage and a portion of the tips they received. Cooks, greeters, etc. also got a part of the tip. Because of their experience as servers, I believe in tipping well. Don't be cheap if the service is good to great. If it's bad, still tip, but maybe understand that your server might just be having a bad day and need to be encouraged. If they are rude...that's a different story.

I have never regretted those times of being generous. I have a huge belief that what comes around goes around. Also generosity is contagious. It just makes our world a better place to live.

Take a look back at how you have taken care of your finances in the past. What's worked? What hasn't worked? What do you wish you had tried? The past is never wasted if we learn from it.

NOTE: Trying to change my financial situation from the past can be like trying to save myself from drowning in the middle of the ocean...it can't be done...unless there is a rescue team. Seek help if you are drowning.

Is your present financial situation stressing you out? If it is, why? And who can help you get over this crisis?

ANOTHER NOTE: It is often assumed that those who stress about money are only those who can't pay their bills. THIS IS NOT TRUE. Even those who have lots of money can be filled with stress that can ruin their own lives and the lives of others. Having a lot of money can be a huge stress factor in people's lives. Lots of money can do strange things to people.

Where do you want to be...a year from now...five years from now...in your retirement years? Is it consistent with your current lifestyle?

AND ONE MORE NOTE: If your financial picture for the future is not good, only one of two things needs to change...your income or your lifestyle.

And now, a word about work:

Work is good. Did you hear me? Yes, work is good. It's not what life is all about, but it is certainly a large part of life. And my attitude toward work is critical. Again, the challenge is to avoid extremes. Hating work or being addicted to work will both lead to a miserable existence. The reality for many of us is that it's never too late to adjust what we're doing or even to change it up completely. That may mean going back to school or learning to live on less. In some cases a lateral move is possible, but that's rare. My financial picture is definitely linked to my work and so choices need to be made.

Just don't procrastinate. Make your decision with the advice of others who are wise (they may not be your best friends) and move ahead.

Remember..."if you love your job, you never have to work a day in your life." And this is when work becomes really good.

WHERE FROM HERE?

...Step One...where do I want to go?

Have Goals...if we aim at nothing...we will wind up with nothing!!! Money drains like water down the kitchen sink. Figure out your top three goals and begin to head there today.

...Step Two...what do I do NOW...the immediate?

At least three possible ways to go from here:

1. Line up an appointment with a financial counselor who has a good reputation. Check references.

2. Pay a bill...it's just good practice.

3. Use your creativity to make a piggy bank and put something in it. And do so every day for the rest of your life. And then if you are really brave, when the time is right, give it away to someone who could really use the help. Or...keep saving until you can afford that SUV with the air-cooled seats.

THE BOTTOM LINE

MONEY MATTERS BUT IT ISN'T EVERYTHING

...AND KNOW IT WILL INFLUENCE YOUR DREAM CHASING TO SOME DEGREE.

1. MONEY PROVIDES THE *INITIAL MEANS* FOR DREAM CHASING.

2. GOOD FINANCIAL MANAGEMENT PROVIDES A **BASIS TO SUSTAIN** MY DREAM CHASING.

3. SAVINGS WILL ALLOW YOU TO **ENJOY** YOUR DREAM ONCE YOU GET THERE.

HERE'S A SUMMATION OF THIS CHAPTER USING AN ACROSTIC FOR MONEY:

M ore is not necessarily better. Large sums of cash can bring ruin.

O wning is a two-way street. Our stuff can wind up owning us.

N otice those around us we can help.

E arn what we get.

Y ield to wise advice.

IN THE RING

1. Which quote do you identify with the most and why?

"Too many people spend money they earned…to buy things they don't want…to impress people that they don't like."

—Will Rogers

"I love money. I love everything about it. I bought some pretty good stuff. Got me a $300 pair of socks. Got a fur sink. An electric dog polisher. A gasoline-powered turtleneck sweater. And, of course, I bought some dumb stuff, too."

—Steve Martin

"Financial peace isn't the acquisition of stuff. It's learning to live on less than you make, so you can give money back and have money to invest. You can't win until you do this."

—Dave Ramsey

"Don't tell me what you value, show me your budget, and I'll tell you what you value."

—Joe Biden

"If you live for having it all, what you have is never enough."

—Vicki Robin

2. Content or discontent...which tent do you live in? What is the primary reason you live here?

3. Do you work with a realistic budget on a monthly basis? Why or why not?

4. Who is or might be someone who could help you become better with your money?

5. How does your financial well-being influence your energy level? What does this tell you about your situation?

6. Are you willing to do whatever it takes to get it together in your world of finances? If you aren't, are you willing to forfeit your dreams because of bad money management? Do you realize winning the lottery is not a realistic part of debt payment?!!! Write out a realistic plan of how you will get your financial picture in a healthy dream-chasing position.

CHAPTER SEVEN

CREATIVITY AND RECREATION

TEA POTS

I am always on the look out for something new and interesting to try. This has led to everything from car-cleaning products that promise to remove scratches, to restaurants that provide a different dining experience, to different places to go for a hike or walk. Last December I did something really "different."

I was going down the street, and I noticed a pottery place in one of the strip malls. I am still not sure what drew me in, but I turned in and drove up to the storefront. I went in and what I saw wasn't really what I expected.

There were different pottery pieces all around the walls of the store, pottery ovens in the back, and in the middle were a bunch of tables where people were painting up a storm. These people included women, children, and a few brave men. I smiled as a lady came over and asked if she could help me. I said I was "just looking.."

And then I saw it! A clay teapot. You see, my wife was looking for a teapot and I thought I could paint her one and make it special. I thought it seemed like a great idea that involved some creativity. In fact, I thought it was such a great idea that I would also paint one for my two daughters and my mother-in-law. Christmas gifts!!!

Okay...so some of you are thinking that is kind of cool...some of you may be thinking, *You did what, where, for who?* Stick with me.

I painted one pot bright-red for my oldest daughter Alyssa, one pot purple for my youngest daughter Arika, one pot white for my mother-in-law, and one pot a pale green for my wife, Cheryl. I spent a few lunch hours working on these projects. My final touch was that I painted everyone's names across the bellies of the teapots before they went into the kiln for the final bake.

The teapots were ready a few days later. I was pleased with the final result and couldn't wait to get the family's reaction.

Oh yeah, there was one more part of this project. On small pieces of paper, I wrote out qualities that I appreciated about my wife, daughters, and mother-in-law. I folded these notes individually and placed them inside the pots.

Part of the challenge was to get the teapots safely from Victoria to Calgary where we were celebrating Christmas. After I carefully wrapped them, I am pleased to say they arrived without incident.

Here were the reactions. My mother-in-law, Moira, loved it and thought it was creative (she is a creative person herself). Arika... my youngest daughter thought it was cool...she liked it...saw it as thoughtful. Alyssa...my oldest daughter was amused...she thanked me. And Cheryl, my wife...well...let's just say she was perplexed. She wanted to be kind...she said it was nice, asked when I had time to do this "creative" work, and bravely said it really wasn't the teapot she was looking for.

And honestly, these were pretty much the reactions I expected. And I was delighted with each response, including my wife's. I knew it wasn't really what she was looking for. Maybe this year I will get her a teapot that fits our kitchen and doesn't have her name written on it (in large letters, I should add).

My point after this long story is this: Creativity is about self-expression and at the end of the day can be extremely satisfying, regardless of the response of others.

Creativity has the power to give us an unexpected injection of life.

And yet, I would say that most people I know have somewhere along the line, lost the necessity to be creative.

Yes...you read right. I said necessity.

I have a strong belief that we have been made in the image of our Creator and that means we have a built-in need to create. Somehow, someway, it is essential that we discover or rediscover what this means for our lives.

When we fail to be creative we will wind up in that one place that can be emotionally crippling. That place is called The Land of Boredom. But when we enter the creative zone, we will find life; a life that has learned to express outwardly what is on the inside. This includes the good, the bad, and the ugly. It includes our realities. It includes our fantasies.

As you have read through this chapter, you've probably had one of two responses:

The first response is that you identify with what I am saying with a resounding, "Yes!" You are either currently in the "creative zone," or have been there before and long to get there again.

Or, you will respond with a, "Huh?" You may be so caught up in detail, routine, and the "shoulds" and "musts" of our crazy culture that you don't think you are a creative person. That is what only the few strange people I know do.

If your response is the latter, let me say that for your own sake (and even for the benefit of those around you), it's time to explore and find what being creative looks like for you.

It may bring you back to life and provide energy as you chase your dreams.

So let's assume you agree with what I am saying here, but your natural response may be that you just don't have time to be creative. Maybe you are a working-outside-the-home, single parent, who is barely surviving. Or maybe there are a number of other demands and expectations that prohibit you from exploring any kind of such nonsense.

On the other hand, you know that if you don't visit or revisit the land of creativity, you will surely die. Oh, you will keep breathing, but there won't be much left of you...the "you" that you know is in there somewhere.

If you have time to watch TV, try experimenting with something that might just get your creative juices flowing. Perhaps have a doodle pad in your hand while you watch your favorite show, and scratch out a picture, a one-word response to what you are watching, or an idea that comes to you. It can be easier to get started than you think.

Perhaps the greatest motivating factor when it comes to getting back on track with your creativity is that you'll find it a great way to relieve stress. It can help to shift gears and prevent mental and emotional burnout. It can take us from a place of exhaustion to a place of re-creation...or recreation as we call it.

Here are a few benefits from discovering energy through creativity:

1. It could lead to meeting new friends or to reintroduce our-selves to others who have similar interests.

2. It will provide us with some humorous moments as we once again learn to LOL at our creative mishaps.

3. Discovery of a new talent we never knew we had could happen.

4. Our minds will begin to think more creatively in other areas as well, such as our work and family life.

5. We may just find our smiles that we had lost through the bumps and bruises of life.

WHERE FROM HERE?

Well...do you want to join the land of the living and actually enjoy life once again? I think most of us long for this. We want to get our creative juices flowing and perhaps even try something we have never tried before.

It all begins by writing out ideas of things you have done in the past or would like to try.

I will give you a possible list...go ahead and add to it. There are few limits when it comes to being creative:

- Build a model

- Draw something just for fun

- Take pictures of things you have never taken pictures of before

- Learn to knit

- Do some woodwork

- Write a poem or story

- Journal using pictures only

- Take a class on something that appeals to your creative self

- Discover that your creative nature is expressed in a sport of some kind

- Start a collection of affordable and interesting objects

...and don't be afraid to fail and simply start again in a new area. If you fail, count it as a unique experience worth laughing about and try again.

Keep in mind that you are the final judge in determining what is creative and re-creative for you. We may ask others for advice or ideas, but it is up to you to go in a particular direction.

THE BOTTOM LINE

It comes down to not just agreeing with this need but to actually finding what we are going to do and yes, doing it.

It means making sure there is room in our schedules for such adventure and knowing this is not an option but a necessity for us and for those we do life with. If we are healthy, our relationships will become healthy...or at least healthier.

So...research, sign up, get out there, acquire the supplies/equipment, and begin to find what you know has been missing

DON'T QUIT ... REST IF YOU MUST ... BUT DON'T QUIT

There may be times when you feel like giving up or have scheduling conflicts. Count on it. Be ready for it. Make up your mind right now that you won't quit. You may need a rest or a break. That's normal. But schedule a date when you will begin.

To conclude this chapter, I want to add another dimension of "re" creation.

It is a big part of the creativity process. It centers around the word rest. Consider the following acrostic:

RELEASE

My wife and I recently went on a weekend trip to Tofino, which is one of the most beautiful places on Vancouver Island. The trip to get there was about four hours by car. During that scenic drive, we were able to **RELEASE** our stressful thoughts and responsibilities. We were able to let them go, even if it was just for a couple of days. But in that release, we enabled ourselves to enjoy the weekend ahead.

ENERGIZE

What energizes you?

The answer to this question will look different for each of us.

If we think that just by going away we will rest, we may be fooling ourselves. You see, even resting well involves good choices (just can't get away from that).

Again, using our weekend to Tofino, we did things that energized us. We ate at a restaurant with great food and a stunning view of the ocean. A walk was in order, so we walked a mile-long beach. We limited our time with our cell phones, which kept us more in the beauty of the moment. We went for a drive to explore the surrounding hotels and towns. And we enjoyed a glass of wine from a special vintage given to us by our daughter and husband at Christmas. Our conversation involved a lot of laughter as we reminisced about things even from our recent past.

If I go to rest on my own, I may find energy by reading a good book at a coffee shop. Walking, listening to music, browsing the Web, and looking at cars I dream about having are also some fun things I do that **ENERGIZE** me. (My wife just doesn't get the car thing.) I also have no problem eating alone in a nice restaurant. (Some of you feel like a spotlight comes on you the moment you sit down...Not true.)

Again, I ask, "What energizes you?" Think about it. Do up a list. Maybe you will find it has been a long time since you have done some of these things. Maybe it's just time to take a rest and indulge yourself.

SLEEP

I usually find a time for an extra nap when resting.

By the way, if you think resting is only about sleeping, you are wrong. A sleep or power nap may provide short-term help, but that's all.

Here are a few things you might find helpful in gaining a good **SLEEP** or nap in a restful time:

1. I have said it before and I'll say it again. Release. You may need to picture yourself putting all your stresses in a bag and tossing them over a cliff. My mind picture involves giving all my cares and anxieties over to God and letting Him deal with them. (This is actually an invitation from the Bible.) Perhaps you simply choose to transition your mind to a happy place from your childhood or from a vacation you once took. Whatever it takes, if you are going to sleep well you will need to let go of troubling thoughts.

2. Consider putting your senses in a good place. I love the sound of rushing water or waves, the scent of fresh air, and a warm blanket on a comfortable bed. For you, it simply might be soft lighting and soothing music. Or a place of complete stillness and quiet.

3. If possible, avoid setting an alarm. Enough said.

4. Finally, when you wake up, focus on something positive. It might involve thinking about an activity or holiday you are looking forward to down the road, or a quote that makes you smile, or a picture of a person that has encouraged you. Avoid thinking about all the things that need to be done that are stressful...at least for a few minutes as you wake up.

TRANSITION

And then, after a time of re-creation, slowly begin to **TRANSITION** yourself back into the reality of life. Begin with a small, easier-to-handle task before engaging in some of the "heavies" of your life. Verbally state (even if you are by yourself) at least one thing you are thankful for about your life. And then take a deep breath, and carry on.

Take a look at two pictures:

"STUCK"

Picture a big ol' 4-wheel drive truck that has done what it has been designed to do; gone off-road and tackled a muddy, sludge-filled ditch somewhere in the back country. (Sounds fun!) Now imagine that the feat has actually become too much for this monster truck to handle. The wheels are spinning, smoke is billowing, and mud is flying everywhere, all to no avail. The truck is stuck.

"BLOOM WHERE YOU'RE PLANTED"

Now picture a desert. Some of you are imagining a huge piece of pie á la mode. No, no...not a dessert... a desert. You know... nothing but sand, sun, and heat. Got it? Okay, now imagine a beautiful, bright-colored flower coming forth from seemingly out of nowhere. By the way, these desert flowers actually exist. Amazing!

Which picture will give you energy to chase your dreams?

The point is this. Many of us are living life in the "stuck" picture. The wheels are spinning, the mud is flying, and we are going nowhere. The challenge is to embrace what can be "desert" conditions in our lives and have the belief that beautiful, colorful flowers can come about right where we are. We can bloom where we are planted. And this is where creativity and re-creation can provide the "assisted living" injection we need.

Which picture will you choose to live in?

Some of you are saying, "I don't have a creative bone in my body."

You are wrong. I challenge you to find someone who used to live with this belief but one day discovered a life-giving creativity gene that enabled him or her to soar...or to see flowers in the desert of life.

Some of you may also be saying, "Not only do I not have a creative bone in my body, but I don't have the time or energy to find an activity that will provide re-creation."

My friend, no matter how busy you are, if you don't find the time and energy or a few minutes of re-creation every day or two, all you will find yourself doing is spinning your wheels.

So please, not only for your own sake, but for the sake of those you love, find that creative genius that really does exist in you and determine that you will embrace **DISCIPLINE AS YOUR FRIEND** and find a way to bring re-creation into your life.

IN THE RING

1. Which quote do you identify with the most and why?

"There is no doubt that creativity is the most important human resource of all. Without creativity, there would be no progress, and we would be forever repeating the same patterns."

— Edward de Bono

"The creative is the place where no one else has ever been. You have to leave the city of your comfort and go into the wilderness of your intuition. What you'll discover will be wonderful. What you'll discover is yourself."

— Alan Alda

"Creativity is inventing, experimenting, growing, taking risks, breaking rules, making mistakes, and having fun."

— Mary Lou Cook

"You can't wait for inspiration, you have to go after it with a club."

— Jack London

"Creativity is…seeing something that doesn't exist already. You need to find out how you can bring it into being and that way be a playmate with God."

— Michele Shea

2. What do you do for fun?

3. Do your tendencies lean toward creativity or recreation? In your mind, what's the difference between the two?

4. When was the last time you tried something new to you that was in the "fun" zone? Describe the experience in one word.

5. Which of the following words are you naturally drawn to? Are you willing to try experiments with the other words? Why or why not? What could that look like for you?

- SPORTS

- MUSIC

- ART

- DRAMA

CHAPTER EIGHT

THE SPIRITUAL

NIGHT OF FEAR

When I was a young kid of about five years old, my older brothers had their turns taking care of me when my parents went out. My youngest older brother often had friends over when it was his turn. Come midnight on Friday nights they gathered and watched movies on what was called, "Night of Fear."

Now these were B movies at best. They had titles like *Wasp Women*, *The Invisible Man*, *The Incredible Shrinking Man*, *Dracula* (Bela Lugosi version), *House of Wax* (Vincent Price), and so on. They were black and white horror movies, with haunting music and lots of shadows and dramatic pauses. I still think they are much scarier than today's overdone horror flicks that leave little to the imagination.

The interesting fact in all of this is that my brother let me stay up and watch. I remember hiding underneath a blanket with eyes closed tight, covering my ears from the music and screams. Something tells me my brother and his friends rather enjoyed my fright.

As a result, I grew up afraid of the dark. These "Night of Fear" events did more to shape my prayer life than anything else! I am the first to say that fear and guilt are two of the worst prompters to discover a relationship with God, but to this day when fear comes, I pray.

Prayer and spirituality are often connected. Prayer has taken on many forms over the years and there are many different understandings of what prayer is and does. Spirituality has become so wide a subject that you never know what you will discover when chatting with people about their particular beliefs.

Think for a moment about the two-dimensional and the three-dimensional. In other words, think about seeing a picture versus meeting someone in person, or watching a movie versus attending a live play. Or think about seeing an ocean paradise in a magazine versus being there to smell the ocean, walk on the sand, and feel the warmth of the sun on your skin. Or think about looking through a brochure for some kind of adventure versus feeling the adrenaline rush and sheer exhilaration of a personal experience.

Let me share something that compares to the last example.

It was in Las Vegas...you know...the adult playground. My wife and I were there with my daughter and son-in-law. We were having dinner together one night when it happened. My son-in-law brought out a brochure of an activity he wanted us to do while we were there. The activity involved going out to place called Exotic Racing. It was out at a Formula 1 type track where we would drive exotic cars. Wow. I was more than ready to participate.

Now, the brochure was filled with descriptive words and cool pictures of exotic sports cars...two-dimensional. But nothing could come close to the actual experience that was to come. I signed up to drive a Porsche 911S, a Ferrari Italia, and a Lamborghini Aventador (700hp).

We went through a classroom-training session where we learned some basic lessons on driving an exotic car really fast. The majority of us had smiles on our faces that would only grow as the time went on. After the session, we picked out helmets and got in line where we would wait our turn to meet a seasoned pro who would join us in the passenger seat to help us out...just in case. The excitement was growing.

The first car I drove was the Porsche. I met my guide, who welcomed me and assured me I was in for one of the most exciting experiences of my life. He was right. He told me these cars were designed to go fast and to hug corners in ways that other cars couldn't.

I started out fairly tame in my approach, but he kept encouraging me to go faster. Each lap was timed. And my competitive nature took over. Incredible. I didn't want it to end. And it didn't. Next I drove the Ferrari. I have never driven a car that even came close to handling like this one did. I wanted one! ...Doesn't hurt to dream. And finally I drove the 700hp Lamborghini.

The instructor told me the Lamborghini has a heavy feel but assured me the acceleration was super smooth. My fastest time was in this car. In all three of these cars I very comfortably drove well over 100 mph into tight corners where near-perfect brakes slowed the vehicle down just enough, and where the paddle shifters easily and quickly allowed for smooth shifting, in order to resume high speed.

SO...other than reliving this experience, I wanted to give a clear contrast between a two-dimensional brochure and a three-dimensional driving experience.

This is the difference between life without the spiritual, versus life with the spiritual – two dimensions versus three dimensions.

There is no comparison.

SPIRITUALITY AND THE MEANING OF LIFE

If you were to describe the meaning of your life in one sentence, could you do it? I'm not talking about someone else's idea about the meaning of your life...I am talking about your description.

I remember being challenged by a college professor to make an effort to define the meaning of my life as it would affect everything else. He was right. Once I could write out and recite the meaning of my life in one sentence, it served to help me develop all other areas of my life with a sense of confidence and purpose.

Here's the thing. The spiritual aspect of my life helped me get to that one sentence. It added another dimension that has made life so much more exciting and worth the living. It doesn't take very long living on this planet to sense there just has to be more.

INSIGHT, GROWTH, MEANING, AND CONNECTION

INSIGHT...GAINING KNOWLEDGE AND PERSPECTIVE

I admit there is a part of me that wants to tell you what I believe, why I believe it, and that you should believe it too. But that would be short circuiting what for most of us is an important part of the spiritual process. I am referring to the searching and learning process.

Included in this process can be listening-to and even debating close family members and friends. It may involve reading books with reliable authors, spending time in thought and prayer, or talking to a counselor or spiritual director to examine and discover a spiritual component in your life.

A word of caution...okay, two words of caution. First, be careful of only using the media as the primary source of information. I am not against the media, I just believe we need to do research and think for ourselves. Secondly, I believe in evil spirits. In fact, one of the reasons I believe in God is because of the wickedness that is so prevalent in our world. So...again...just be careful. If there is someone or something you come across that is telling you to hurt yourself or others, or to control or abuse others, I suggest you should move on ASAP.

GROWTH...FROM HERE TO THERE

As long as I am alive and have a mind that works, I always want to learn and grow. I never want to be a "know it all," who claims to have all the answers. After all, how can a " know it all" learn? I desire to hear different ideas and opinions and want to apply as many helpful ideas into my life as possible. This may mean change.

Don't be afraid to change. Learn to embrace that which may be for your own good. And if it's for your own good, it's usually good for others as well...especially those who are closest to you and whom you love the most.

MEANING...INTERNAL WORKINGS

Then there is the constant striving to understand the meaning of life. I know many who have given up on this subject. They just don't really care. Survival is good enough. But it really is hard to live day after day without some kind of meaning. Even if there are times when I say, "My meaning today is to make it through another day."..there will be other times when I need more than that. I need a meaning that leads to a purpose to keep me breathing day after day.

CONNECTION...GOD AND OTHERS

It has always been one of my greatest motivations to develop spiritually because I believe it is possible to connect with God. Many reading this book might say they have had experiences where they believe beyond a doubt that they connected with the Creator. And these moments take us to new heights in our lives and journeys as we move forward.

How about the spiritual aspect of relationship with others? Have you ever had a best friend, a connection, or a dynamic between you and another person that has gone beyond the norm? Probably more women would admit to this than men, but it can be a really good thing. I fear many of us men are too busy pretending we have it all together, and we won't let our walls down long enough to become vulnerable to one another. Been there, done that, and believe me, that is a huge mistake.

Maybe you have been hurt badly in a relationship and just aren't willing to go there again. Consider this. I said it earlier. Everything in life that is worthwhile will come with some kind of risk. If you want to have a relationship with God and deeper connections with others, it will mean stepping out in faith...a faith in more than just yourself.

WHERE FROM HERE?...LOOK IN, LOOK UP, LOOK OUT!

LOOK IN

What's going on the inside of you?

We have become a culture of critics. We know all the problems with politicians, athletes, actors, friends, family members...etc. What we aren't very good at is critiquing our own lives. It is so much easier looking outward than it is to look inward.

However, if we are going to chase and achieve our dreams, it is essential that from time to time we do a gut check...or more specifically, a heart check.

Now and then when I am meeting with people, I will ask them how they perceive the color of their hearts. This is an exercise I put myself through occasionally, to help understand what going on inside me.

I share a color comparison that would roughly sound like this...

GREEN - growing and learning

BLUE - sad and maybe struggling with depression

BLACK - skeptical and maybe even cynical

BLACK AND BLUE - full of hurt and pain

YELLOW - enthusiastic about life and the future

WHITE - blank slate open for new adventures or ideas

RED - healthy, loving, and peaceful

You get the idea. And through this process a person can at least begin to identify where he or she is and start a process of improving the color if need be.

LOOK UP

Who cares enough to help you?

This is a really important question if you are going to find someone in a higher-up position who can assist you in the inner workings of your heart and life.

This may wind up being a family member, a good friend, a counselor, or someone who has helped you in the past, such as a mentor. You may need to think this through carefully, depending on how much changing or healing needs to take place.

I do want to share my deepest belief. God not only cares about your life and your heart, but He loves you. One of the most powerful phrases from the Bible I cling to is this: "If God is for us, who can be against us?" (Romans 8:31). I have so many stories about how God has demonstrated love to me and to those I know and love. Anyway...I feel a sermon coming on, so I will "back away from the pulpit."

By the way, I am a follower of Jesus. The reason is simple. I need ... absolutely NEED lots of mercy and grace in my life. And the essence of Jesus's message is hope in a God who has more mercy and grace than I could ever use up.

The way I understand mercy is that it frees me from my mess-ups thanks to forgiveness.

My understanding of grace is that it enables me, by God's strength and wisdom, to make the most of my God-given life.

...Okay...so I just had to preach as I was backing away... :)

LOOK OUT!

How do you know when things inside are healthy?

Tough question to answer. But one way to find out if your heart is healthy is to check your relationships.

Here are some diagnostic questions that could help:

Do I tend to lift people up or bring them down?

Do I believe that every person really does have a "10" on his or her forehead and that it is my job to help bring that number up especially if he or she is living like a "5" or less?

Is the bitterness of unforgiveness rotting my soul? Is it time to forgive and let go? (By the way, you do know that unforgiveness can destroy your life, while the person who hurt you may care less if you forgive them or not. Forgiving is something we do for ourselves. It may lead to a new start in a relationship, or it may not. But forgiving may break chains that are holding you back from even dreaming, never mind chasing a dream.)

Is there someone you need to let go of?

Is there someone you need to talk to and set boundaries with, who needs to let go of you?

If you were to put out one request to God for your life, what would it be? Are you willing to be vulnerable before God?

My last word on this topic of spirituality is based on one of the most familiar and powerful psalms from the Bible. (It was written by King David, who was a shepherd at one time in his life.)

Here it is:

"The Lord is my shepherd, I lack nothing.
He makes me lie down in green pastures,
he leads me beside quiet waters,
he refreshes my soul.
He guides me along the right paths for his name's sake.
Even though I walk through the darkest valley, I will fear no evil, for you
are with me; your rod and your staff, they comfort me.
You prepare a table before me in the presence of my enemies.
You anoint my head with oil; my cup overflows.
Surely your goodness and love will follow me all the days of my life,
and I will dwell in the house of the Lord forever."

Psalm 23:1-6 NIV

My favorite line has always been...

"HE REFRESHES MY SOUL."

My soul...my heart...my inner spirit...gets messed up from time to time. Knowing the Lord can do something for me beyond my own ability, is the ultimate meaning of saving grace....YEP...had to preach...it's my calling.

High-octane fuel is designed to make engines run cleaner and perform better. I have also heard it said that it will extend the longevity of the motor train.

Having a healthy spiritual life will enable you to chase your dreams with excellence. It will provide premium fuel. "Those who hope in the LORD will renew their strength. They will soar on wings like eagles; they will run and not grow weary, they will walk and not be faint" (Isaiah 40:31).

Don't ignore what just might be the most important injection of energy you could ever hope to find.

IN THE RING

1. 1. Which quote do you identify with the most and why?

"You are one thing only. You are a Divine Being. An all-powerful Creator. You are a Deity in jeans and a t-shirt, and within you dwells the infinite wisdom of the ages and the sacred creative force of All that is, will be and ever was."

> — Anthon St Maarten, *Divine Living: The Essential Guide to Your True Destiny*5

"Before you find your soul mate, you must first discover your soul."

> — Charles F. Glassman, *Brain Drain The Breakthrough That Will Change Your Life*6

"There are two types of seeds in the mind: those that create anger, fear, frustration, jealousy, and hatred and those that create love, compassion, equanimity, and joy. Spirituality is germination and sprouting of the second group and transforming the first group."

> — Amit Ray

"In all circumstances, we must let God be in control. He is able to guide us in the best pathways."

> — Lailah Gifty Akita, *Think Great, Be Great!*7

---

5 St Maarten, Anthon. *Divine Living: The Essential Guide to Your True Destiny.* Indigo House. 2012

6 Glassman, Charles F. *Brain Drain The Breakthrough That Will Change Your Life.* RTS Publishing. 2009

7 Akita, Lailah Gifty. *Think Great, Be Great!* Create Space Publishers. *2015*

"Your heart has a deeper intelligence than your mind ever will."

— Eileen Anglin

"I have come that you might have live to the full."

— Jesus Christ

2. Who do you admire as a "spiritual" person and why?

3. What is your view and understanding of God? What is your primary source for information?

4. What do you think is the difference between religion and spirituality?

5. Which of these two...religion and spirituality...best describes your upbringing? Which of the two best describes where you are presently?

6. How does your current spiritual condition/practice influence your energy level?

CHAPTER NINE

MOVEMENT

ACTION, CEMENT SHOES, AND TENACITY

ACTION

"BLAH, BLAH, BLAH BLAH, BLAH!!!"

...If there is one thing that we are not short on...it's words.

A good part of my profession is listening. I hear people complain about their circumstances. I hear people criticize others. I hear people filled with blame as to why they are in the state they are in.

I also hear a lot of good intentions. People have plans and know exactly what to do to make life better. There is absolutely nothing to be said to "know it alls."..simply because in their minds...they "know it all."

Then there are those who have plans, have good intentions...and actually follow through with faith and action.

It is these people I admire and serve to inspire.

Years ago I developed a friendship with someone who had every reason to curl up and die. Life had not been good and certainly had not been fair. He had been on his own as a young teen. Parents had disappointed him. And he wound up in an unsuccessful marriage.

But...he was a live-and-learn kind of guy and was aware he had much to work out and work through.

He got a counselor, developed a life plan, and embraced an "I can do it" mindset. As a result, he has built a beautiful home, furthered his education, is successful in his career, is building a fulfilling relationship, and lives to do the best with what he has.

ADVANCE

When I get up in the morning, I generally have goals I want to accomplish during the day that somewhere fit in with my life plan. These goals are checked on throughout the day to see if progress is being made. Before I go to bed I see how I've done. I don't beat myself up or make a big deal of small defeats or victories. These goals, which I usually have on the notes on my cellphone are simply indicators.

Even if I am able to reach one of my goals per day, I know I am moving in the right direction.

DEALING WITH THOSE "IMMOVABLE" MOMENTS

The reality is that we all have those times when we just seem to be stuck. The mud (or snow) is deep and wheels are spinning.

In those moments we may feel like just giving up. It is at these points in life that finding a way get "unstuck" will make the difference in moving ahead with our dreams.

CEMENT SHOES

EXCUSES, EXCUSES...

There can many reasons we get stuck. It could be a health-related thing that has taken precedence over everything else. Maybe a crisis has demanded your attention and all you can do is deal with what's in front of you. Even those moments when those close to us are in great need and we have to help them out, can leave us stuck with regard to our own life plan for a period of time. When these things happen, tend to them, and then resume your life-plan development.

BUT...distinguish between reasons and excuses:

Let's face it. Often we have more excuses than reasons for not chasing our dreams and moving ahead with our life plans. Excuses suck. I have no other way of putting it. I firmly believe that people grow miserable because we become our own worst enemies. I know that when I get grouchy or down, it's usually because I have excused away something I really need to do. Most of our problems in life are our own doing. And most of our problems are not because of good reasons but are due to lame excuses. I think you know the difference. Honestly...at the heart of excuses is laziness or insecurity. And laziness over the long haul can ruin a life.

Assuming you are willing to quit letting yourself off the hook, you can now get out of the mud.

Here are a few suggestions:

1. Improve Traction

Growing up in prairie snowstorms meant getting stuck every now and then. At times all it took was using a piece of material, or at other times some sand for better traction would help. Another solution was to use a shovel (or facsimile) to dig the snow away.

Sometimes when we get stuck in life we are able to find our own way out. It may take some creativity, but it can be done when the mud or snow isn't too deep.

2. Get a Push

On cold, snowy winter days there were often Good Samaritans who stopped, got out of their own vehicles, and offered a push out...Sometimes it took a number of Good Samaritans.

It has surprised me that when I've gotten stuck in life, I have seen a number of Good Samaritans come around to help. The help may have been as simple as words of encouragement. Sometimes it has been practical ways of helping. There have been so many times when I couldn't have gotten out of the muck without them.

3. Find a Pull

On occasion, the right person at the right time with the right tools comes along. I have heard stories about when someone has gotten stuck in a ditch somewhere, a person with a truck comes along and pulls them out with a winch. These individuals are more than Good Samaritans...they are angels.

It doesn't happen often, but sometimes when all I have done and all those in my world have done to help isn't enough to get me out of the mud and mire (and yes, snow) of life, someone comes along out of the blue, who is especially well-equipped to help me. I can think of at least one instance in which I was stuck in self-pity, when a book with a "specially equipped" author pulled me out of my plight. It was a pull and a kick in the pants from... the right book, written by the right person at the right time with the right tools.

4. Hire a Tow Truck

Sometimes the most expensive and time-consuming option is the only choice.

It is just a fact that there are times in winter snowstorms that "all the king's horses and all the king's men" can't get the vehicle out of the snowbank. That is when a call is made to a tow truck company who, for a fee, will come to the rescue. But in a snowstorm, be prepared for a wait. You aren't the only one looking for help.

I am so thankful for paid professionals...doctors, counselors, and teachers...who from time to time are there to help me when I am stuck and nothing else will serve to get me unstuck. I have been so blessed to have had great professionals, who have been the difference-makers in my getting back on track and moving ahead. However, know this. Those who are really good at what they do will be in great demand. Therefore, be patient and do your best in the meantime.

TENACITY

I have mentioned my dog, Tessa. And let me tell you, she is one tenacious Yorkie. Especially when it comes to "breeder approved" bones about the size of her head. Once she gets one she will stay on that thing until it's so small we take it away from her so she doesn't choke on it. I guess that's where the saying, "Like a dog on a bone comes from."

We have all seen it and we dare not try to take the bone away from a dog that has it in its grip.

This is a great example of tenacity and how we have to be, if we are going to be successful dream chasers.

TENACITY DEFINED

te·na·cious: adjective \tə-ˈnā-shəs\

: not easily stopped or pulled apart : firm or strong

: continuing for a long time

: very determined to do something

HOW DO I BUILD TENACITY INTO MY LIFE?

Mindset

We have already talked about the power of our thoughts. I cannot emphasize enough how important it is to place a thought in our minds as to where we want to go and then keep it there. We may experience challenges and problems along the way, but if we are stuck on a thought excuses will disappear.

Say it

That's right. Say it. Once you have written out a dream, a life plan, or even a simple goal say it out load. Say it to yourself. Say it to someone who will keep reminding you in a timely fashion of what you said. I used to think this was pointless, but I have learned there is something about verbalizing thoughts, goals, and dreams that helps make them stick.

Act

The first step in the right direction is critical. But...so is the second step, the third step, and so on. The truth is that we get to where we want to be one step at a time. And each step is necessary. The key is not to focus on all the steps that need to be taken but rather to keep our eyes on the purpose of the next step. That will give us the fuel to move forward.

Prepare for and learn from mistakes

How does one prepare for mistakes? Isn't that self-defeating?

Absolutely not.

What this means is that we accept mistakes as part of the process, recognize the poor decisions we've made, define them as best we can, learn from them, resolve not to make the same ones again, and get up and keep going. A mistake only becomes a failure when we give up.

Celebrate victories

Note what I said. Celebrate "victories." If we celebrate too soon or reward ourselves too often along the way, we will slow down and may even come to a halt. Have you ever seen a football player begin to celebrate before he gets across the goal line only to lose the ball and face humiliation? Point made.

Learn to anticipate rather than expect

Over the last few years, this has become an important part of my thinking.

There have been times when I have lived my life expecting all kinds of results that never took place. The result was disappointment.

Then I made a slight transition. I began to anticipate the unknown with a sense of faith. The reason for this is simple. Often when I anticipate that the unexpected will actually help me chase my dreams and enable them to become a reality. BUT when my sometimes unrealistic expectations aren't met, it can bring me to a grinding halt.

Enjoy the trip

I am sure you have heard this in different ways in your life. It's a fact that some of us get destination fever and think that we will only be happy when everything is perfect or we actually achieve our dreams. I hate to ruin the party, but...

I learned a long time ago to embrace each day as a gift and strive to live life to the max. And how you do that is something you are going to have to figure out. Just be aware that if you are making headway toward your dreams, all is well.

AND FINALLY...

...Never give up or DIE TRYING.

I told my son-in-law, Paul that I wanted to die trying to achieve the dreams in my life. He smiled and told me about a screen saver he had seen on his boss's computer. It said this...

I hope you will never give up on chasing your dreams.

IN THE RING

1. Which quote do you identify with the most and why?

"Several excuses are always less convincing than one."

—Aldous Huxley, *Point Counter Point*

"Hold yourself responsible for a higher standard than anyone else expects of you. Never excuse yourself."

—Henry Ward Beecher

"Whoever wants to be a judge of human nature should study people's excuses."

—Hebbel

"I attribute my success to this: I never gave or took an excuse."

—Florence Nightingale

"The trouble with always leaving yourself a way out is that you always take it."

—Robert Brault, rbrault.blogspot.com

"He that is good for making excuses is seldom good for anything else."

—Benjamin Franklin

"If you always make excuses to not follow through you deserve the weight of anxiety on your chest."

—Daniel, @blindedpoet

"A man can fail many times, but he isn't a failure until he begins to blame somebody else."

—John Burroughs

"The best day of your life is the one on which you decide your life is your own. No apologies or excuses. No one to lean on, rely on, or blame. The gift is yours – it is an amazing journey – and you alone are responsible for the quality of it. This is the day your life really begins."

—Bob Moawad

"Sometimes I wish I had a terrible childhood, so that at least I'd have an excuse."

—Jimmy Fallon

"The best way to overcome excuses is to quit using them."

—anonymous

2. What is your "go to" excuse for not chasing your dreams? Is it an excuse or a reason? What's the difference? List other excuses you have become good at using to keep sabotaging yourself.

3. What is an excuse you have put behind you to succeed or move ahead? What was the key in overcoming the excuse? How did it influence your overall attitude?

4. What is an area of your life in which you have chosen to never give up? Write a paragraph stating what that area is and how your sticktuitiveness has influenced you and others.

CHAPTER TEN

PRICE CHECK

DETERMINING WHICH DREAMS ARE WORTH CHASING

I like shopping. I know most men aren't crazy about this activity unless it car, tool or sports-equipment shopping. I'm not really sure why I like it, other than the fact that as I was growing up my mom and aunt would take me to downtown Regina to shop every Saturday. Ultimately we would end up at the café in Kresge's department store for a Coke and fries.

As time went on, I went shopping with my friends. We took the bus downtown, bought some hockey cards, and played pinball at an arcade. Then when we got our licenses, we would go to malls and record stores. It was just a part of growing up.

Cheryl and I always include shopping on our vacations. For some reason, we find it relaxing and enjoyable. However, as time has gone on, my wife enjoys it less and less, leaving most of the shopping, including grocery shopping to me. And I'm okay with that.

On occasion I come across an item that doesn't have a price-sticker, located in an area without signage or clerks. It is then that I go looking for one of those devices, usually located on a post, which scans a barcode and provides the price information. Sometimes, even though the price is on an item, I will still scan it just to see if there is a sale price I am unaware of.

You've probably done the same.

Whether or not I buy an item is based on two things. First, is the price fair, and secondly, how bad do I want it. There are times when the scanner tells me the item is more than I want to spend, but I want whatever it is so badly, I buy it anyway. Then I go home, usually regretting that I paid more than I initially was willing to pay.

This is not unlike what happens when we dream chase. I sometimes want a dream so badly that I pursue it and only later realize that the cost was greater than I thought. This can have all kinds of consequences. This chapter is dedicated to considering the cost BEFORE I chase a dream. There can be few things worse than chasing a dream and then realizing the cost may lead me to bankruptcy. And I'm not just referring to finances.

COUNTING THE COST OF A DREAM

TIME

We get one shot at this thing called life. There are no redo's, mulligans, or backspace buttons. If only! Have you ever said something and immediately wished you could have retracted the comment? We all have. Once it's out there...once it's said...no erasing it.

Life is a gift. And in every phase of life we have choices that will free us to become better dream chasers or will chain us down. One is an energy boost...the other drains our energy.

Consider these three important time zones:

The Past - Though it is true we can't go back, we can learn from the past. Our success and failures are our greatest teachers. In fact, our failures probably teach us more than anything else. IF we pay attention to what is being said through them.

Here are some valuable lessons I have learned from the past:

1. As an extrovert, I have learned the hard way that every thought I have doesn't have to be expressed verbally for all to hear. It's okay to keep certain thoughts to myself.

2. Don't love someone according to what your love language is...find out his or her love language and proceed accordingly. Thanks to my dear wife for teaching me this...

3. Choose friends carefully. Not everyone is going to help us in chasing our dreams. There are people who lift and people who lean. As I look back I have learned that that not everyone is good for me.

4. The only really appreciable assets we have are people. I say this during a time when I am thoroughly enjoying and investing in my grandchildren. This, my friends, is what legacy is all about.

5. Get a variety of input for your dreams and ideas, and at the end of the day weigh it all out and make a decision you can live with. Don't be a people-pleaser to the extent of sacrificing what you were created to do. Serving and helping people is good. Succumbing to the pressure of others who wish to control us, is not.

The Present - All I truly have power over is the given moment. Therefore, strive for peace, learn to enjoy moments throughout every single day AND make wise choices. Be careful of whims and desires that could hurt others and ruin your life. I believe a life is made up of living each day in freedom and embracing every opportunity to do the good that needs doin'. This produces energy to dream chase without regret.

I never used to be a morning person. Morning people seemed strange; overly happy and optimistic. And then I realized that's not a bad way to live. About twenty years ago I started getting up before anyone else in the household to read my Bible and other books of hope and encouragement, and to pray. This is where I learned to live open-handedly. This meant releasing my anxieties into the hands of God, receiving the mercy and grace of Christ, and relinquishing the temptation to control things or people that are not mine to control. I cannot begin to tell you how this has made my present moments more enjoyable than ever. Life is way too short to be grumpy, angry, bitter, mean, guilty, oppressed, judgmental, cynical, depressed, anxious, controlling, or addicted to energy killers such as junk food, alcohol, drugs, porn, television, too much sleep, "couch"itis, or whatever else there may be that is holding us back from missing out. A good start to a day can go along way to living a healthy existence.

The Future - Determining what lies ahead involves daily choices that will need occasional tweaking. This is where you get to determine which dreams you will chase.

Of course, there is so much about the future that we don't know. There will always be things like hard-to-face doctor appointments, accidents, turns in relationships, job changes, etc. However, we can choose to coast and let life happen or find a dream worth chasing and get on with the adventure.

Imagine that at this very moment someone gives you a blank page and a pen and asks you to write out the top three dreams that you are desirous of and capable of achieving. Now prioritize these dreams according to desire and achievability. AND NOW, consider which dreams may cost you more than what you are willing to spend, lose, or give up. Having a hard time getting these three dreams in proper order?

You're not alone. Keep reading...

RELATIONSHIPS

Family - Counting the cost at this particular point will depend on where you are in life. Hoping to someday have a family of your own? In the midst of raising your kids? Maybe you are an empty-nester with some time on your hands. It could be that you are in the pre- or early retirement stage and your children are self-sufficient and busy living their own lives. Or maybe you are a caregiver to a family member. All of these stages of life involve family to some degree. Here are some important questions that need to asked:

1. Am I willing to give up some family time to chase my dream?

2. If I am in a committed relationship, is my spouse or partner willing to release me to spend the time it will take to chase my dream?

3. Can my family be a part of my dream chasing?

4. Am I willing to put my dream on hold or even to let go of it if a family member needs me to be there for him or her?

5. Will the achieving of my dream, should that happen, benefit my family and their overall happiness?

I'm sure you are getting my point. How's the prioritizing of those dreams looking now?

Friendships - On a scale of 1-10 (10 being highest priority), how important are your friends to you? This is a multifaceted question. For instance, if your friends are partnering with you in your dream chasing, at what point are you willing to be released from your dream to save the friendships? If your friends help you with your dreams, will you help them? Do you understand that if you pursue a particular dream that your usual recreational time with friends may have to take a backseat for a period of time?

Personally, I have always placed a 8-10 value on friends. Their roles in my life have served to give me honest feedback (no patronizing with good friends), and often my friends have come alongside to help me any way they can. I see friends as a huge part of the dream-chasing process.

And you? What is the role of your friends in your life? Have you thought about that in the prioritizing of your dreams?

HEALTH

Physically - How in shape are you? I didn't say "what" shape are you in, I said "how in shape" are you? A lot of our dreams will take physical exertion of some kind.

First, do I have the physical energy it's going to take to ensure I won't wear out? Have I prepared for the journey ahead and am I continuing a discipline that will help my strength increase over time? The reason for this question is that if we exert energy it is imperative that we build up a reservoir to keep us from hitting empty on the fuel gauge.

Secondly, do I have a physical limitation of some kind? If this is the case, I will either have to forfeit a dream, adjust it so it fits, or get help from someone who can do the physical things I just can't do. This could be as simple as finding someone to help me do heavy lifting if I have back issues.

If I don't consider the physical costs of my dream, down the road I may face the consequences of chronic pain or be forced to withdraw.

Our physical health is just something we have to think about when it comes to dream chasing.

Mentally - If I am going to chase down a dream, I ought to consider my brain capacity. Here are some helpful questions:

1. Do I have enough room in my head to put yet another idea that will need plenty of attention? Is this really the time?

2. Do I have the smarts it's going to take to move my dream down the road? At what point will I need other people's smarts? Plan for that at the beginning of your dream process.

3. Is there a book, a course, a website, a mentor that I need to tap, in order to provide the knowledge and insights I must have if I am going to build and sustain my dream?

4. Do I know myself well enough to determine the difference between a verifiable dream and a fantasy? Chasing a fantasy usually ends in disaster.

5. Who do I know that will tell me the truth about my thought process and whether or not chasing this dream is really a good idea? My recommendation is that you talk to at least three people who know you well enough to challenge you in your thinking. Remember to listen without defense. Listen to all three and then take some time to consider what you have heard.

Emotionally - Dreaming can begin by releasing endorphins that make you happy and excited. Dream chasing on the other hand can bring stress/anxiety, times of discouragement and disillusionment, and moments where we are simply flat-lined on an emotional level. That's not to say there aren't moments of sheer exhilaration, but unless we are up to handling the difficult times, we may just crash and burn...which isn't good for anyone.

Some might say that if you are already going through a stressful time, the last thing you need is another challenge in your life. Rather, I have found that when I have other pressures and emotional pain, dream chasing can be just what I need to keep me breathing.

One of the most emotionally trying times in my life came when my mom died. I felt alone. She had been the one who was my greatest cheerleader and prayer warrior. In her eyes, there was nothing I couldn't do. Suddenly she was gone. I still grieve this loss some fifteen years later.

I had some choices to make. Do I do the symbolic "climb into bed and pull the covers over my head" or do I keep reasonably active, even to the point of continuing to dream and dream chase? I made the second choice. I kept active, led the church I pastored with renewed vigor, and saw a time of substantial growth. My dream chasing helped me heal.

Spiritually - The questions I ask on occasion are these: "Where is God in the midst of my dreams and dream chasing? Does he really care what I do with my energy and time? Can I involve him in my dream chasing?"

I personally believe God does cares about what I do with my energy and time when it comes to dream chasing. I believe running my thoughts by him is never a bad idea. In fact, for me to pursue my dream with a clear conscience, I even believe that his involvement is a must. Consider three verses from the Bible that are a personal guide to me.

"Commit to the Lord whatever you do and he will establish your plans."

—Proverbs 16:3 NIV

"If any of you lacks wisdom, you should ask God who gives generously to all without finding fault, and it will be given to you."

—James 1:5 NIV

"I can do everything through him, who gives me strength."

—Philippians 4:13 NIV

I have mentioned that I am a Christ follower and thus believe the Bible. This book has helped me on more occasions than I can even begin to recount.

What is your source of spiritual strength and inspiration? Has it stood the test of time? Is it trustworthy? Has it proven to lift you up in your greatest time of need?

I hope we all understand the importance of counting the cost of dream chasing and believe that we will need outside help...beyond the smarts and strength of the mere mortals. Spiritual health can make the difference in finding what it takes to press on.

MONEY

What Do I Have? - First stop in this process...your bank account. If your dream chasing is going to cost you dollars, then you need to be prepared. This may include being responsible to the point of paying off existing debt.

It may also mean considering those who may be dependent on your income for their basic needs.

There are times when dream chasing has start-up costs. In the long run, is it worth taking out a loan or using a line of credit?

At what point do you say enough? Setting a budget is critical if you are to move ahead without getting yourself and maybe your family into trouble.

What Will I Need? - Big picture thinking will require the help of others.

This involves thinking beyond start-up costs to see what will be needed as the dream grows and involves more resources.

Depending on what your dream is, consult someone who has travelled this road before and learned a thing or two financially along the way. This may even mean hiring a consultant or business coach. You could save yourself a fair amount of cash if you find the right person to help.

Will There Be Any Return? - Will the result of my dream chasing be:

A. A constant drain on my bank account

B. Self-sustaining over time

C. Income

D. Not sure

Think about this over a period of the next year...two years...and five years. What is the best-case scenario? What is the worst-case scenario? What is the probable scenario? Be honest with yourself. Avoid Fantasy Island and the world of negativity. At the end of the day, just be prepared. And at this point, count the cost of your dream chasing...literally.

REPUTATION

At what point do I need to care what others think? - This is a question few think about when it comes to the cost of dream chasing, and yet, it's important to ask at the beginning of the process.

If chasing down your dream involves sacrificing your character and relationships to get where you want to go, pick another dream. On the other hand, accept that not everyone is always going to be happy with you and that's called life.

I believe it is possible to keep your reputation intact and achieve a dream. It may mean being patient and doing things with consideration, but in the long haul you will make others proud of you and you will feel good, not only about fulfilling a dream, but more importantly, about who you are as a person.

LEGACY (THAT WHICH I TRULY LEAVE BEHIND)

Here are some key words when it comes to our legacy:

Priorities - Can you name, in order, the top five priorities in your life? Are those closest to you convinced those are the order of your priorities?

Influences - How have you influenced the people who matter most to you? What have you taught them about living a life that matters?

Character - Who are you when no one is looking? I have heard it said that the most difficult person one will ever lead is oneself. The proof of leading myself effectively comes when I can be alone and know that there are ongoing improvements in my character. If character qualities such as love, patience, kindness, generosity, integrity, humility, and consideration are being formed within, then I am leading myself effectively. If I am bitter, greedy, full of myself, rude, selfish, and cynical...time to get help. I have lost control of my life.

In my profession, I have been around many who are in the final stages of life. Most I have known take extra care to make sure their wills are in order and that everyone is treated fairly. When they die, they are aware that they will leave behind some kind of inheritance.

Some have failed to realize that there is something more important than leaving money behind. That something is legacy. Legacy is not only a will, it is a lifetime of stories and relationships that have revealed our character. And our characters leave deeper impressions than money does, with regard to the life we have lived.

I recently received an inheritance from my aunt. She was very generous to me and my brothers. We appreciated her kindness. But what I often remember about my aunt, is that she was a survivor through some difficult situations in her life. She was my mom's best friend and loved us boys as if we were her own. You see, she never had children. So we were it for her. And her life has inspired me to never say, "I give up." She could have said that many times in her life, but instead of getting bitter, she got better. And even at the end of her life, she kept striving toward personal growth on a number of levels. She died at age eighty-one.

In your dream chasing, consider your legacy.

In fact, do more than consider your legacy. Make a good legacy a part of your dreaming. Perhaps it is the dream that is worth chasing the most.

AND NOW...ONE LAST BIG QUESTION WHEN IT COMES COUNTING THE COST OF A DREAM AND USING UP FUEL IN YOUR ENERGY TANK:

HERE IT IS...HANG ON TIGHT!

IS THIS MY DREAM OR SOMEBODY ELSE'S DREAM FOR ME?

The only person who can ever answer this question is you.

Where are you in this? Do you own your dream? Is it a dream you are sharing with someone? Or are you slowly becoming embittered with chasing something that really isn't yours to chase?

Be careful with this. It has teeth. Maybe it's a subject I can address in another book.

Stay tuned.

"POST"AMBLE

The difference between a "pre"amble and a "post"amble is that the former deals with the mindset one has going into a literary work and the latter deals with the afterthoughts once the book has been read.

The main thought I want you to embrace after completing this book is that you will never have enough FIYT to chase your dreams on your own. YOU NEED OTHERS.

Years ago, I remember taking an anthropology class. I remember how the professor, who had multicultural experience, told us that we Canadians were not the norm when it came to how we do life here in Canada. He shared how other cultures, especially those in third-world countries, live communally more than living the individualistic life that most North Americans lead. Though intellectually I understood his point, I really didn't get it until I visited places in South America and Africa. I was able to see and experience first-hand what it meant to accomplish life together.

In the late 'nineties I was in Bogota, Colombia. At the time it wasn't a particularly safe place to be. I went with a group of Canadians, many of whom were tall males with fair-colored hair. A missionary lectured us about the recent kidnappings of people from North America, which was related to the oil industry.

He told us that we were all at risk except for...me. I carry a year-round tan and I am on the shorter side. He told me I could pass for a local.

This opened the door for me to go to places others weren't allowed to go...such as open markets, neighborhoods, schools, and certain street locations.

As a result, I saw life lived on a different level; a level of family, community support, and connection not usually seen in my Canadian environment. People were far behind in daily earnings, services, conveniences, and privileges. But they knew how to stick together.

Having *F*uel *I*n *Y*our *T*ank is not nor will it ever be just dependent on you. We are meant to help one another achieve our dreams.

If this is the One Thing you have learned or relearned while reading this book...you are better off for it.

NOW GO...AND CHASE YOUR DREAMS!!!

LIFE PLAN TEMPLATE

MY LIFE PLAN

NAME:

DATE:

PURPOSE: (one sentence that clarifies your reason
for living)

VALUES: (core principles that influence your character and
choices ie. honesty, kindness, generousity, tenacity...)

PRIORITIES: (top 5)

1.

2.

3.

4.

5.

GOALS: (measurements that will be governed by your purpose, guided by your values and determined by your priorities ie. "I will talk to someone in my area of interest by the end of the month")

INSPIRATION: (people, quotes, sayings, pictures * 'attach')

ACCOUNTABILITY: (person/people, methods, ways, that will hold you to what your purpose in life is, who you have determined to be, where you have decided to go, and how you plan to get there)

WRITTEN-OUT INTENTION: (prayer of intent, commitment, surrender and need for outside strength and wisdom)

NOTE: once you have completed your life plan, share with at least one other person.

PICTURES THAT ADD FUEL TO MY TANK

HOCKEY-PLAYING GRANDSON

FAVORITE PEOPLE IN MY FAVORITE PLACE

FRIENDS WHO ARE THERE WHEN YOU NEED THEM

A LITTLE UNASSUMING CHURCH WITH A BIG HEART

THE OCEAN

"ALL IN" COWORKERS

CHICAGO BLACKHAWKS

"HELP OUT" TRIPS LIKE THIS ONE TO THE CONGO

TESSA THE THE THREE LEGGED WONDER DOG

SACRED SPACE

JUST FOR FUN...

GO OVER YOUR PICS ON YOUR PHONE, FILE, OR ALBUMS AND SEE WHAT PICTURES MAKE YOU SMILE AND WHY. WHICH PICTURES ADD FUEL TO YOUR TANK AS YOU CHASE YOUR DREAMS?

SEND A PICTURE TO SOMEONE YOU KNOW AND LOVE, WHICH WOULD ENCOURAGE HIM OR HER TO CHASE DOWN HIS OR HER DREAM

SOME SONGS THAT ADD FUEL TO MY TANK AS I DREAM CHASE:

1. "Runnin' Down a Dream"

   Tom Petty

2. "Right Now"

   Van Halen

3. "Fire It Up"

   Thousand Foot Crutch

4. "Trenches"

   Pop Evil

5. "What Are You Waiting For?"

Nickelback

6. "Could Have Been Me"

The Struts

7. "Get Over It"

Eagles

8. "Confident"

Demi Lovato

9. "Stick to your Guns"

Sick Puppies

10. "Oceans (Where Feet may Fail)"

Hillsong

11. "This Is Not a Test"

TobyMac

12. "A Change Would Do You Good"

Sheryl Crow

WHAT WOULD "YOUR" FIYT SONG LIST BE?

FIYT MOVIE LIST?

FIYT PEOPLE LIST?

FIYT VACATION SPOTS?

AUTHOR

Randy Rohrick is a dream chaser. His life purpose is to make the most of his God given life. Besides his love for hockey, dogs, classic rock, traveling, shopping, dining out, writing, and hanging out with friends and family, Randy has attained his motorcycle license. His newest love is riding his Harley Davidson around the winding roads of his home on Vancouver Island in British Columbia. He lives near Victoria with his wife, Cheryl, where he provides soul care to a great group of people at Westshore Alliance Church.

CPSIA information can be obtained
at www.ICGtesting.com
Printed in the USA
LVOW06s0407121116
512509LV00003B/5/P

9 781460 287811